cancer, covid and me

Cancer, Covid and Me

MARISA WRAY

Published in the United Kingdom in 2022
by Marisa Wray using Kindle Direct Publishing

10 9 8 7 6 5 4 3 2 1

Text copyright © Marisa Wray 2022

ISBN: 9798442341393

Cover picture by BSGStudio downloaded with commercial license from buysellgraphic.com and modified by 42 Creative
Typeset in Garamond size 12
Printed in the UK by Kindle Direct Publishing

Like me, many will have felt the impact of COVID-19 on absolutely every aspect of life. This book is for those who know the agony of waiting, those who have the good fortune to be both a doctor and a patient, and those who seek to understand their cancer diagnosis and their treatment.

CONTENTS

APPENDICES

ACKNOWLEDGEMENTS

My biggest thanks go to Steve, my husband, for sticking with me through the turmoil of having cancer during a pandemic. Your endless love and care keep me going. Thank you to Victoria, Steve's daughter, for being a wonderful part of my life.

Thanks to Mum and Dad, Nick, Di, Jess, Michel, Lal and Mario for pulling out all the stops for me. Thank you for loving me and for making encouraging noises at each chapter I sent you to read as they poured out of me.

Thanks to Martin, the oncologist, without whom I would never have found Hospital B and the excellent care I received there.

Thanks to Mr T and the breast care nurses from Hospital B for your sterling handiwork and for telling me off for wanting to climb Helvellyn too soon.

I'd also like to thank the surgeon and breast team at hospital A for being so understanding when I transferred my care. It wasn't your fault – Hospital B was just resuming surgery a bit faster.

Thanks to Merryn for being such an incredible support and for showing me the strength within myself I never knew I had. Your guided meditations were the difference between me sinking and swimming. Thank you for your care in editing this book!

Thanks to Jude, my counsellor from Cancer Care. You were a complete star!

Thanks to Ali for telling me to rest. You may have saved my implant from wound dehiscence and ultimate implant loss.

Thank you to all my colleagues who were so supportive during my torturous wait for surgery when I was at work in body but not in mind. Particularly Amanda for asking how I was doing and showing astonishing insight. Thanks Alison N, for agreeing to fund a locum to cover while I took time off for surgery – it meant that I felt far less guilty for leaving the team and my consultant colleague in the lurch.

And finally, to my readers, thank you for reading, thank you for listening, thank you for just being.

PREFACE

I am just one of an estimated 2.3 million women worldwide who was diagnosed with breast cancer in 2020, during the coronavirus pandemic. My diagnosis was perfectly timed to coincide with the first UK spring lockdown, when the NHS (National Health Service) appeared to become a COVID-19-only service. I was one of the lucky ones: lucky that as a doctor, I knew where to turn to expedite my treatment, and lucky that my cancer was caught early. I continued to work as a consultant old-age psychiatrist in a community mental health team in the Lake District in the UK, all the while knowing I had a tumour growing in my breast, which I could do nothing about.

This is not a story about a warrior (I hate that term!) who came through against all the odds. It is simply an inelegant account of something I was not expecting, which hit me slap in the face and left me reeling. If it helps just one woman affected by breast cancer to know that she is not alone then it will have been worth sharing.

PART I

THE CLIMB

Chapter 1

My Bleeding Nipple

Wednesday 12 February, 2020
I'm undressing for bed. That lovely pyjama feeling. Hmm that's odd - is that blood? Ew!

'Look,' I say to Steve, my husband, who's already climbed into bed. 'My nipple's bleeding.'

There's a dark stain in my bra too. Did I squish my breast too hard against my bag strap when I was hurtling down the cycle path on the way to the Med School yesterday? Oh well, that's weird but it's probably nothing.

Saturday 15 February, 2020
My left nipple is still bleeding at night when I press on it. I'd better get it looked at.

Monday 17 February, 2020
10:25
Steve's voice drifts in from the kitchen. 'Love, have you called the GP?'

'Oh yeah, forgot yesterday. I'll message them today. It's that online system. You can't get an appointment anymore, it's all via email and text.'

OK, better find my login for Ask My GP. At least this way I don't have to hang on the phone for ages listening to pre-recorded messages and getting cut off when I press the wrong button.

10:48
I begin to fill in the blanks on the Ask My GP online appointment system.

This is about a: New medical problem

Your request in a few words: Bleeding nipple
Who would you like help from? Dr Crabtree

Hang on a sec, computer says no! Dr Crabtree doesn't seem to be available in the dropdown menu...

> **Who would you like help from?** Anyone
> **How long have you had this problem?** 5 days
> **Please describe your symptoms and any idea of the cause. What are your concerns today? How would you like us to help?** I have a small amount of blood that oozes from my left nipple when I press my breast around it. It is dark red but does not appear to contain pus. Painless, no palpable lumps and no lymphadenopathy [swollen glands]. I have done a literature search and narrowed the differential diagnosis down to intraductal papilloma or duct ectasia [small, wart-like growths in the breast ducts, or widened ducts which can fill with fluid. Both are benign and the most common causes of nipple discharge]. I know breast cancer is way down the list but want to rule it out. I think it is most likely to be a side effect of HRT.

My medical students would be proud. I practised what I preach: the art of condensing a disparate array of symptoms and experience into a coherent whole and I'm rather pleased with my little clinical summary and formulation.

10:55
Yes! A reply from Ask My GP.

> **Due to overwhelming demand, we are now fully booked and will struggle to respond to your request today.**

That's fine. Not urgent. It would make more sense to speak to Dr Crabtree about it anyway because I consulted her for the HRT (I put both breasts and HRT under 'women's stuff').

10:59
I see another reply from Ask My GP.

Dr Crabtree is in tomorrow. We will pass this request to her and she will be in contact with you.

Nailed it! Thanks to my succinct history and differential diagnosis (what's likely to be wrong with me, given the signs, symptoms, my age and medical history). Tick, job done. Now I can forget about it. Trouble is, it's not about one of my patients. Of course, it's not urgent, it can wait until the GP is in tomorrow. I might not have bothered if I didn't have to report back to Steve.

Tuesday 18 February, 2020
09:08
I have a message from Ask My GP.

Good morning, Marisa. Unfortunately, due to unprecedented demand over the past few days, Dr Crabtree has reached full capacity already today. She is next available on Thursday. We will forward this request to her that morning and she will be in touch with you to discuss this further. Please accept our sincere apologies for the delay in dealing with this for you.

Ah well, no bother. They'll get to me eventually. Too busy to be dealing with this anyway.

Thursday 20 February, 2020
09:00
Today is Thursday, clinic day. Trouble is the medical school has thrown a spanner in the works: this is the only day they are able to hold the exam board so I'm here (medical school) instead of there (clinic), where I should be seeing patients. Sigh! My day is planned almost down to the minute given that I'm supposed to be in two places at once. It would be lovely to have a TARDIS.

As I'm only here one day a week, I don't qualify for a parking permit and I'm too stingy to pay. So I park on the muddy verge near the nature reserve, and slip and slide up the 'path' to campus. At least I get to stretch my legs.

11:00
Why is it so hard to concentrate when you know you need to be somewhere else? I have to leave by eleven forty-five at the very latest.

11:45
I'm on my way back to the car, my head filled with the names of students who have failed their formative exams.

Erm, what time's my first patient in clinic this afternoon? Can't remember whether it's a complicated case or not. Probably is. They wouldn't be seeing me if it wasn't.

I check my emails as I walk. Bingo! A message from Dr Crabtree via Ask My GP.

Hi, I just tried ringing both numbers and have left a message on your mobile. Please let me know when you're free and I will try again. Kind regards.

How sweet of her to be concerned. Normally if you miss their call, you have to start the request all over again.

12:00
I'm getting into my car and my mobile's ringing. By some miracle, I answer before it goes to voicemail. A breathless voice says, 'Hello, this is Dr Crabtree. I only saw your query today. It's not something we can just leave. I don't need to see you, I'm sending a referral to breast clinic right now. Oh, and you'd better stop the HRT.'

Yeah, fine. Oh, hang on, I'm going on holiday in just over a week. Bad timing! Oh well, let's wait and see what they come up with. Doubt I'll get an appointment before we go away anyway.

16

13:00

I'm in time for my afternoon clinic, if not for lunch.

In between patients, my phone rings again. It's the appointment clerk from the breast clinic. Wow, that was quick! There's an appointment available on the twenty-seventh. That's Thursday next week! OK, yes, I'll take it!

16:30

I put my apologetic face on as I sidle into my secretary's office.

'I'm going to be a pain again, I'm afraid. You'll have to rearrange next Thursday morning's clinic too. I've got a two-week-wait appointment at breast clinic.'

Silence. Look of horror. 'Oh, is everything okay?'

'Oh fine, I'm sure it's nothing. Had a bit of bleeding from my nipple. It's probably just the HRT. Appointment's at ten and once they've checked that everything's fine, I should be out within a couple of hours. So, I should be safe to see my first patient at one. I'm sure they'll expedite me in and out if I tell them I'm a doctor and I've got my own clinic to go to.'

Before I know it, both secretaries are sharing their own experiences of having had a 'scare' and a visit to breast clinic: 'They're very efficient there, you know. They give you a mammogram and a biopsy, and they let you know everything's normal that same day! You'll be fine.'

Chapter 2

Breast Clinic

Thursday 27 February, 2020
09:30
Ooh, I can park in a red permit space! The perks of being a consultant: a priority parking permit. No one will know I'm a patient and not a doctor today.

I'm nice and early. It's a beautiful sunny day and I'm enjoying walking around the hospital grounds listening to the birds singing. Oh, what time is it? Was it such a good idea to arrange a Skype meeting with a student at nine forty-five when I'm due in breast clinic at ten?

Phew, I've got a signal.

The conversation goes well. What a lovely student.

09:58
Right, let's get this over with because I need to be out by a quarter past twelve at the very latest. I told my medical student to meet me at twelve-fifty. Hmm, maybe that was a bit optimistic.

Erm, where *is* breast clinic? I've never needed to know where it was. Lucky I'm very early - I've just done a whole loop of the hospital on foot and not found it. Better call and ask. Ah, it's not even in the main hospital building - that's where I went wrong. Out on a limb here near the visitors' car park… Found it!

10:00
I'm sitting in the waiting room. It's a light, not unpleasant-looking room with big windows and different-sized bays. Magazines abound and a coffee machine stands in the corner. Quite modern. I'm feeling positive. I hope no one minds that I just bought a huge cup of coffee from the staff canteen. This is weird. Am I the

youngest here? Actually no, there's a much younger woman over there in a tracksuit and trainers.

Most people seem to have come with either a carer or a partner. I brazenly look around at people who avoid my gaze and try to imagine what they're here for.

10:05

'Marisa Wray!' I stand up and smile. Wow, maybe I'll be out of here by twelve after all! Spoke too soon. I've just been ushered into another waiting room.

'Wait here, please.'

This one is windowless and rectangular, a niche within a corridor containing multiple consultation rooms. Nurses bustle purposefully to and fro without meeting my eye. I admire the paintings by a local artist, hung to try to mitigate the starkness of the setting.

10:15

I'm sitting topless on the couch in the doctor's consulting room. She presses on my left nipple which obligingly discharges bloody liquid. She remarks that it's reddish-brownish-yellow. Nice!

'It's just a side effect of HRT, no?' I ask.

'No, HRT doesn't cause nipple discharge. There are several causes of nipple discharge, one of which is cancer,' she explains.

I can't imagine I've got cancer… nah. I've already diagnosed myself with intraductal papilloma or possibly ductal ectasia. That's the most likely, isn't it?

10:45

This is a novel experience. I'm not old enough to qualify for breast screening, yet here I am face to face with the mammogram machine.

The mammographer is very kind and gentle, and warns me that my breasts will be very squished in the machine. She's even trained in positioning me in just the right way. I joke that my boobs are so small, there's barely any boob to squish. Is it easier

19

with larger breasted ladies? Apparently so. It must be much more rewarding to have a bit more flesh to work with!

Both breasts get squished in the horizontal then the vertical plane so nothing is missed. Well, that did a good job of expressing all the blood from my left nipple. Sorry about the mess!

Back to the waiting room. Hmm, something's wrong. Those nurses who wouldn't meet my eye before as they bustled past are now smiling at me and giving me looks of such kindness it makes me blush.

Would I like a cup of tea? Why not. It passes the time. Am I likely to be here much longer? They're not telling me anything but their looks say it all.

I call my secretary. 'Hi, I'm really sorry about this but it looks like I might be at breast clinic for some time. Can we put my one o'clock patient back a bit?'.

Ugh, when am I going to make up the clinic time? Stress! Calm down. Book a holiday.

11:17
I text Steve.

> Hi Love. Am at breast clinic waiting for tests. Am amusing myself by looking at flights to Salzburg. They have come down a bit to total £532. What do you think? xxx

> **Yes, better price Love. Victoria got 2 2:1 and 1ˢᵗ xxx**

Victoria is Steve's daughter. She's in her final year of a psychology degree in Liverpool.

> Well done Victoria! Will txt her. Should I book?

> **What happens if we pay then there are travel restrictions?**

> Um – I'll look into it.

How will I pass the time? I vaguely recall marking an exam question about breast cancer where the answer was 'triple assessment'. That's what I'm getting today! I google it. The three parts are clinical examination, imaging (mammography and ultrasonography) and histology (biopsy). Am I in for the lot? Right, what time is it? Eleven thirty. They'd better hurry up. I look around. What is it about inner and outer waiting rooms? I got all excited when they ushered me into the inner sanctum, but now I'm getting used to hearing 'Sit down and wait here.'

I study every detail of the paintings on the wall and run my phone battery down by playing solitaire and impulsively googling all aspects of breast cancer diagnosis.

12:00

The ultrasonographer is fascinated by my mammogram. That's not good. I was hoping it would be normal and I could go home. She does an excellent job of explaining that there are segmental pleiomorphic calcifications which look rather pesky and need biopsying. 'Look at all those little dots and lines, all different shapes and sizes, in the upper, outer segment of your left breast. Your right one looks completely normal by the way.'

Ultrasonographers use a *lot* of gel. I'm covered in the stuff. She has a very sure hand and I trust she knows exactly what she's doing. She explains that the calcifications are widespread but also disparate, so they are going to take a core biopsy from three separate areas. She also identifies two 'masses' that look like liquid so she sticks a needle in and pulls some yellow fluid out of each. They shrink down to nothing. They were just collections of tissue fluid.

I'm classified as P2, M4, U3. P stands for clinical examination, M for mammogram and U for ultrasound. I will get a B (biopsy) score once the histology has been done in the pathology lab. I google the triple assessment again and find out that the ratings go One (normal), Two (benign), Three (uncertain), Four (suspicious of malignancy), Five (malignant). Figure that! So, appearances are benign, mammogram looks suspicious for malignancy and

21

ultrasound is hedging its bets. I guess I average a Three. Great - neither here nor there!

12:27

Turns out I'm not an easy case. Nothing is ever straightforward.

Oh heck, I'm supposed to be running a clinic in half an hour! I'm not going to make it – and no one can tell me how much longer I'm going to be here. I've already rung my secretary to ask her to put my first appointment back to two but it doesn't look as though I'm going to make that one either.

I apologise profusely to her (again). I feel awful about letting my patients down. Still, I'd far rather get all the tests done today than have to come back another time (especially as I'm about to go on holiday).

I'm feeling very discombobulated now but a bit calmer. Things are out of my hands so I might as well relax. I'm not the only one in a pickle. Opposite me in the inner waiting room is a girl (I call anyone who looks my age or younger a girl) in floods of tears, talking on the phone about having to postpone her clinic. 'You too?', I sympathise. She's a GP practice nurse and was due to start her clinic at one. Join the club. What a palaver!

13:00

I'm learning first-hand about ultrasound-guided core biopsies. They sample area A six times. Not to worry, the local anaesthetic stings a bit but after that I feel nothing other than a bit of pressure, and I hear a satisfying 'click' each time another chunk of breast tissue is chomped out by the biopsy needle.

After a bit of discussion, they're not happy to leave it at that. They want me to have a stereotactically guided biopsy (or two) just for good measure. Those calcifications are so widely distributed that they need to know exactly how to get at the outer margins of the abnormal area. Am I OK to stay a little longer? Sure! Since I cancelled my clinic, I've all the time in the world.

13:36

I'm back in the inner waiting room. I carry my shirt and keep on the front-fastening surgical gown which covers my pin-cushioned breast. It's very quiet as we're in the hiatus between morning and afternoon clinic. Can I pop out to get some lunch? I'm starving! Apparently not. I'm supplied with a lovely cup of tea and I succumb to scoffing biscuits (on my blacklist of edible items).

The lady sitting opposite smiles at me. I smile back. 'I never thought my boobs were big enough to cause me this much bother!'. We have a bit of a giggle. You gotta laugh, haven't you? Otherwise you'd cry.

14:30

Well, this is very high-tech. Thankfully the trolley bed on which I'm lying is reasonably comfortable because when they position me in the scanner, I can't move a millimetre.

My poor bruised boob is being well and truly squashed and mauled flat as a pancake so they can identify the right areas to sample. Now, when they said they were going to do three biopsies, what they meant was they were going to chomp six chunks from area A, nine from area B and fifteen from area C. It's a wonder I've got any breast left.

Apparently, I bleed a lot and am going to have some spectacular bruises tomorrow. I now also have three metal clips in my breast to mark where they took the tissue from.

'Don't worry,' I'm told, 'they won't set the airport machine off.'

15:05

I send another text to Steve.

Hi Love, still waiting. Had to cancel my afternoon clinic. Will call you when I get out. xxx

OK Love. Wish I was with you. xxx

You'd be terribly bored! All very nice here though. Wasn't expecting it to take all day! Just waiting to see the doc. xxx

15:30
I've been sitting in the doctor's office for fifteen minutes. No doctor. I wander out into the corridor. Erm, when can I go?

15:32
'Oh my gosh, we forgot about you!' the doctor exclaims when she catches sight of me. 'You're our longest stay patient today.'
She apologises profusely for having forgotten me.
I'm to come back for the biopsy results in about a week. The lady at the desk will give me an appointment. That's all she can tell me at this stage. Might be something, might be nothing. Well no, it's definitely not nothing but the histology will tell us whether it's malignant or not.
I know it's unlikely for someone my age. But then, that mammogram... and the looks on everyone's faces... Deep breath.

15:40
The lady at the desk offers me a results appointment for Friday next week.
'Can we go for the following Monday as I'm on holiday next week?'
'Sure,' she replies, and books me in.
A little niggle in my mind questions whether I did the right thing to prioritise my holiday over my results. I'm so desperate for a holiday, I don't even want to contemplate curtailing it.

15:45
Driving home, I feel like I'm in a parallel universe. Did I really just spend all day at breast clinic? What should I say to Steve? I could pretend that everything's fine but then I think he would smell a rat. Plus, it's not fair to him to keep things from him. I just want to enjoy our holiday! Why did I choose to go to breast clinic today? I could have spent the holiday in blissful ignorance and gone afterwards.

I feel tired, worn out, emotional. Just want to hide. Don't want to face Steve. Feel like I need to cushion him from this. Bear it myself... spare him hurt and pain. Is that possible?

My mind is working overtime. I'm an observer of reels of video tape, sputtering and changing from one horrible scene to another. I wonder how the NHS death in service contract works? I need to update my funeral plan; it's been a while since we wrote it. My life insurance should pay out... OK, don't get carried away here! One step at a time. Steel yourself until you know what this is, then deal with it. It'll be fine.

16:30
'Hi Love,' I say with a sheepish grin on my face as I walk in the door.

Steve gives me a big hug.

'Ooh, ow be careful, the local anaesthetic is beginning to wear off!'

The entire left side of my chest is swathed in the most enormous bandage you've ever seen.

'I knew it! I had a bad feeling. I sensed that I should have come with you. Why on earth does this have to happen to you?'

I sit and face him across our home office. Does he want me to explain what I found out and what my thinking is? Of course he does.

Deep breath.

'So, to start with, they didn't think it was anything to worry about because the doctor couldn't feel anything when she examined me. But then when they did the mammogram it all changed. The look on the nurse's face just said 'cancer'. My left breast looked really abnormal - it was full of calcifications. It's not normal to get that many. The radiographer showed me the picture - they were everywhere. My right breast looked completely normal, thank God. The doctor said the HRT couldn't have caused it - I wasn't on it for long enough. So, they took lots of samples. It's tricky because when there's such a widespread area of abnormal tissue you don't know if you've got the worst bit to sample or not. It's like looking for a needle in a haystack. That's why my breast's been pulverised! Now we just have to wait for the results.'

Oh hell, I feel like shit.

17:30

Thursday is stir-fry night. Prawn crackers followed by prawns and veg in black bean sauce, with loads of ginger and enough garlic to keep the vampires away. And a bottle of wine between us. Boy, I need some wine! But before we eat, I need to know what I'm dealing with.

I read some papers on interpretation of calcifications on mammography (how good it is to have the whole of Medline at your fingertips when you work for a medical school!) and decide the picture that looks most similar to my own is the one that corresponds to invasive ductal carcinoma. Oh, pants!

My computer won't let me on the imaging system from home. I'll have to look at it at work tomorrow. I justify this by pointing out to myself that the radiographer showed me my mammogram pictures, so I'm sure no one will mind if I take a sneaky peak myself.

18:15

I Facetime Mum.

'Hi Mum, how are you?'

'Are you OK darling?' she immediately wants to know.

I swear she has a sixth sense when it comes to her children.

'Oh yeah, I'm fine. I've just spent the whole day at breast clinic. I didn't tell you beforehand because I thought it was going to be nothing and I didn't want to worry you.'

'Oh darling, did you find a lump?'

'No, my nipple was bleeding so I got it checked out and my mammogram was really abnormal – it's my left breast. They took some biopsies and I'll get the results in just over a week.'

'Over a week! That's far too long! Mum protests. 'You should go private and make sure you get the results ASAP.'

'Erm, I'm not sure that's possible. They have to slice the tissue up and stain it and stuff. It takes a few days and it's nearly the weekend. Plus, we're on holiday next week. I mean, they did offer me an appointment next Friday but that would mean shortening our holiday.'

'Are you mad? Shorten your holiday! You need the results as soon as possible so either they put your mind at rest or you can make a plan. Promise you'll call them in the morning and get your original appointment back.'

Silent groan. 'Steve said the same thing. It's just... my holiday... OK, I know you're right. I don't think I'll be able to relax until I know anyway.'

Sigh!

18:55
I send a WhatsApp message to my sister, Laura, in Milan.

Hey Lalsie, you asked me to let you know how breast clinic went... I have some highly suspicious looking calcifications which are quite likely to indicate cancer. Will get results next Friday. Trying not to think about it in the meantime! Xxx

Oh Misie! Do you have time for a quick FaceTime?

Yes.

I have Maria rolling around but Sara is in bed. Will whisper.

Maria, nearly four, and Sara, fourteen months, are my Italian nieces.

19:25
I'm on WhatsApp with my sister, Jessica, in New York.

Misie I'm worried about you. Are you ok? Mum told me you were waiting for test results?

27

I'm fine... quite likely I have breast cancer but will know more next Fri. Hope it doesn't stop me coming to visit!! Xxx

I'm due to fly to New York on the first of April for my yearly visit to immerse myself in family life with my niece (Yasmina, seven) and nephews (Gabi, five, and Alex, two).

What sort of breast cancer? If you have breast cancer I am coming to you!

Had a load of biopsies today so not sure but they will do histology and got results appointment next Fri. Worst-case scenario it's a mastectomy and chemo. Didn't look like any lymph nodes were involved. May even be benign.
I'll be praying Misie. Keep me posted on everything pls. I love you so much.

Thanks Jessie. Going to cook a stir-fry now. Love you too. xxxxxx

21:33
I receive a WhatsApp message from my brother Nick's wife, Di, in Surrey.

Mis, Nick just spoke to your mum and he's left me a message saying you've had a biopsy? Are you ok? Sorry if we aren't supposed to know or got the wrong end of the stick but I couldn't ignore it. Really hoping everything is ok? Xxx

Hey Di. Yes, left nipple started bleeding about 10 days ago so spent the day in breast clinic. Mammogram highly suspicious so have had about 20 biopsies in the hope that whatever it is will show up under a microscope. Results next Fri. Cancer highly likely but not certain. I feel fine, other than having a pincushion for a breast! Steve in a worse state than

28

me... I'm quite philosophical really. Just deal with whatever comes! Thanks for asking. xxx

Oh my goodness Mis, that's shocking. I don't know what to say apart from I wish I was there to give you and Steve a hug. How are you coping with having to wait until next Friday? That feels like a long time to me?

We are going to Aviemore on Saturday so am determined to enjoy holiday as much as we can!

Good re holiday and I'm sure you and Steve will walk and walk and walk which is good for the body and soul. Still a horrible wait for you and we will keep absolutely everything crossed and pray they find a different explanation for you. Xxx
PS: you actually wouldn't want me there to hug you. Lucy's school closed at lunchtime today until Wed at earliest as 5 cases of scarlet fever, 2 chicken pox and norovirus spreading like wildfire through the forms. Lucy has just started 😫

Lucy is my thirteen-year-old niece. Her brother, Tom, is eleven. That makes seven nieces and nephews altogether.

Oh no poor Lu! Not coronavirus then?

We have been told emphatically that they have no coronavirus cases or suspicions! I will be amazed if that doesn't change...

Lal reckons it's much more widespread than the authorities are letting on...

Wouldn't surprise me tbh. Anyway, missed the bowl this time so I'm off to clean the carpet! Take care Mis and

enjoy your hol as much as you can. Loads and loads of love. xxx

22:00
Finally, bed. I feel mentally and physically drained as I slip beneath the duvet. Ow! I can't lie on my left side - my boob's too sore. I wonder if I'll sleep?

Friday 28 February, 2020
08:00
I think I slept a bit at least. Have to get up and go to work – I've got my appraisal today. Don't quite feel like my mind and body are in sync… am just going through the motions.

The sky is a glowering grey and the heavens open as I drive up to the hospital. The weather's mood is congruent at least.

09:00
I'm in my car at the hospital car park. Right, first thing's first. Call breast clinic to ask for my original appointment back.

I get passed from pillar to post but eventually get through to the person who organises breast clinic follow-up appointments. Yes, there is still space on Friday. Phew! I feel a bit relieved.

09:31
I text Steve.

> Hi Love have rebooked breast appointment for 10:30am on Fri. Love you xxx

09:35
I break the news to my secretaries.

'Can you let the team know that I'm here but I'm not sure I'm really here? I'll be hiding in my office.'

I'm sitting in my office staring at my mammogram. I show one of my colleagues for good measure.

'Oh, bloody hell!'

30

'Mmm,' I muse. I have lots of pretty pictures from papers on characterising breast calcifications open on the screen. 'Don't you think mine looks most like that one?' I ask her, indicating the picture corresponding to invasive ductal carcinoma.

11:30
I need to do something. Need to move. Need to talk. Who can I talk to who'd understand? Oh, my French friend, Josie, who lives up the road. She had breast cancer. She'll know just what this feels like. Right! Action!

11:36
I send a WhatsApp message to Josie.

> Salut Josie. Tu peux m'aider je crois, ou au moins sympathiser. J'ai passé toute la journée hier à la clinique du sein. Mammographie suspicieuse et 20 biopsies plus tard, j'ai rendez-vous pour les résultats vendredi prochain. On part en Ecosse demain pour quelques jours de vacances. Si tu es chez toi en ce moment, est-ce que je peux te rendre visite? Pas de problème sinon. Je dois partir pour mon évaluation professionnelle à Barrow à 13h. Merci! Marisa x

It translates to:

> Hi Josie. I think you can help me, or at least sympathise. I spent all day yesterday in breast clinic. Suspicious Mammogram and 20 biopsies later, I've got a results appointment next Friday. We're going to Scotland tomorrow for a holiday. If you're at home at the moment, can I come and see you? No problem if not. I have to leave at one for my appraisal in Barrow. Thanks! Marisa x

12:08
Yes! Josie says come over!

12:14
I'm sitting in my car outside Josie's house. Better let my boss know what's going on, it's only fair.

12:15
I email my line manager, clinical director for older adult psychiatry.

From: Wray, Marisa
To: Alison
Subject: RE: Self-isolating

Hi Alison,

I spent all day yesterday at breast clinic and have some highly suspicious calcifications which warrant further investigations. They have taken 20 biopsies and I have results clinic next Friday. I hope that I will get some clarification then as to whether I will need surgery. Chances are that I will as if biopsies are inconclusive, they will want to surgically biopsy the whole area, If it is malignant, I will need a mastectomy.

Wanted to give you the heads-up just in case.

I am on holiday next week, back at work on 11 March.

BW
Marisa

12:18
Seeing Josie is wonderful. I sit in her kitchen and drink tea and pour my heart out. She listens. I even learn a few cancer-related French words! Thank God for lovely friends.

14:00
I text Steve.

Hi Love, just arrived in Barrow for my appraisal. Hope your day is not going too badly. Will txt you when I'm leaving. Raining v heavily but roads ok so far. Love you. Xxx

Don't get me started on the doctor's yearly appraisal and five-yearly revalidation system in the UK. Every year, all doctors spend their weekends and evenings (and in my case, annual leave) collating and uploading evidence of everything we ever did onto the online appraisal system. We have to log every course we attend along with a reflection on what we have learned, show evidence of quality improvement activity, gather feedback from our patients and colleagues, declare any incidents, complaints and compliments, and swear that we are honest doctors. We then have to satisfy the General Medical Council by linking every entry to the domains of Good Medical Practice, finishing with a flourish by reflecting on the whole lot.

We all moan that it came about because of a serial killer, the famous Harold Shipman, who used his status as a GP to surreptitiously murder many of his patients. The General Medical Council says it's a myth but the irony is, were Shipman to have had an appraisal, he would've passed with flying colours! More recently we've had to share our patient mortality figures so maybe he'd have been caught out after all. You'll be pleased to hear that my figures are within the norm!

One thing appraisal does achieve for me is help me monitor my own health. It makes me ask myself, 'Where am I, and how did I get here?' Well, regarding my career anyway. I am in the not-so-unique position of being a psychiatrist who suffers from a mental illness. I have always been blessed with very helpful and understanding appraisers (who are fellow doctors). They manage to strike a balance between being challenging yet supportive of both my professional development and my mental health.

It's a miracle really that I made it as far as being a consultant psychiatrist in the NHS. I come from a family of teachers and lawyers, and was the first in my family to pursue a career that was even remotely scientifically orientated. I found medical school incredibly hard, especially the clinical years. I wondered whether I was cut out to be a doctor because although I was undeniably bright, speaking to patients made me really nervous. I was exceedingly shy as a teenager – I wouldn't say boo to a goose. By necessity, medical school knocked this out of me, but I always felt like I was a square peg in a round hole.

After one year of working as the most junior of junior doctors, I escaped to France for a year to do a master's degree in theology and to lick my wounds. Wounds partially healed, I decided to give doctoring one more chance.

My first six months as a junior doctor in psychiatry was a disaster. I hated it. That was it – I decided doctoring definitely wasn't for me. At age 27, I found myself back in Oxford, enrolled in a PhD with a former supervisor from my medical student days. Trevor always said that I was the most productive undergraduate who had ever worked with him, and that he'd be delighted to have me back for a PhD!

My three years as a PhD student marked a turning point for me because during that time, I discovered what I suffered from was not a lack of moral fibre but a recurrent depressive disorder. A friend of mine, who was a consultant psychiatrist, suggested that I go on antidepressants. These turned my life around. For the first time ever, I felt I could cope with life. It was the difference between night and day, and the sun came out. I was able to enjoy things again, the paralysing anxiety was gone, and I felt optimistic and capable. Towards the end of my PhD, I decided to give being a doctor one final try.

Fast forward sixteen years, and here I am, a consultant old-age psychiatrist. I found my niche on day one of my return to clinical work in an Older Adult Community Mental Health Team. I won't say that everything has been plain sailing since I came to terms with the fact I have a mental illness and have been taking antidepressants. Far from it! However, medication, psychotherapy and a very understanding workplace has allowed me to find a portfolio medical career that suits me. My first few years as a consultant were challenging and I discovered I was unable to work full time. Too much clinical work caused me to have a depressive relapse. In my first two years as a consultant, I spent a total of six months off sick. Since going part time in 2012, I have not had a single day off with depression. I find that combining clinical work with medical education allows me to stay well (as long as I take my antidepressants).

15.15
I still feel in a daze but we just got through the appraisal in record time and my appraiser even takes some tips from me on how to prepare to make it a relatively painless exercise. The preparation wasn't painless though. I'm so thankful it all had to be completed two weeks in advance (before the bleeding nipple), otherwise I think I'd be having a meltdown.

17:00
I'm back home and packing for Scotland. I can't believe we're going away. I want to go but I also feel a distinct lack of enthusiasm for energetic pursuits. I feel worn out. Emotionally drained. Ah well, a change of scenery will do us good.

Chapter 3

Head for the Hills

Saturday 29 February, 2020
09:00
I shut the car boot and jump into the driver's seat. I love the Cairngorms. Especially in winter - walking in snow with crampons on and ice axe at the ready. So why do I feel so disinclined to assault the snow-clad mountains this time? My usual vigour seems to have left me. OK, let's take this one step at a time. Do we want to go? Yes. Is it booked and paid for? Yes. Will it be lovely? Yes! Does it matter if we don't conquer any summits or do anything dangerous and daring? No. I know that I will enjoy the five-hour drive, listening to Radio 2, car-watching and making frequent coffee stops. Will sitting at home feeling sorry for myself and waiting for my results appointment help? Emphatically no!

OK, let's go.

17:00
Ooh, it's nice to be at our rented cottage. Let's light the fire and open the wine! I check the forecast. Right, what shall we do tomorrow?

Sunday 1 March, 2020
11:00
Well, I never! We actually made it up Meall a' Bhuachaille (Herdsman's Mountain in Gaelic). I love this walk because it's doable in bad weather and takes in some fabulous landscape.

'Look, we're having a lovely time,' I imply as I ping a photo of the sun and snow and blue sky and mountains and pine trees to the family WhatsApp group.

12.20
We stop off at the Ryvoan bothy, a small stone building nestled in between mountains. We pay a visit here most years. It's basic but it's dry if not warm. It's a place for exchanging stories with fellow wanderers and taking a short respite from the elements, before zipping up our jackets and venturing back into the wilderness.

There are some embers still alight in the tiny wood burner, an unusual luxury in a bothy, and a bit of wood lying next to it. Steve opens the burner, gives it a stoke and places the wood inside. A glow starts to emanate from within.

Mmm, warmth! Another group of walkers arrives, and we swap tales and give advice about the route up the mountain before heading off for lunch by a frozen loch.

16.40
As we make our way back to the car via Lochan Uaine, I somehow manage to push my cancer-horror waiting machine to the back of my mind. I make an extra special effort to notice the scenery and the snow crunching under my feet, and to not let the feeling of dread impinge on my every moment. My God it's tiring enjoying yourself when you've got something constantly trying to assault your thoughts.

Tuesday 3 March, 2020
19:00
I've surprised myself with how much we've managed to do despite everything. We've lunched in a natural snow hole in Coire an Lochan, with the wind whistling overhead; circled the sparkling waters of Loch Morlich; and stumbled upon the hut deep in the Rothiemurchus forest where Mikel Utsi dwelt with his reindeer, reintroducing them to the British Isles in 1952.

I'm so glad we came. I'm sitting in our cosy rented cottage trying to paint the scene of the northern corries, which I photographed earlier today. We discovered snow drifts up to our waists and shared a good giggle and a long walk. Can we do something big tomorrow? I'd love to go up on the plateau. Shall we have an early start and see how far we get?

I'm almost starting to relax. Last full day tomorrow. I can cope better because I haven't got so long to wait for my results now.

Wednesday 4 March, 2020
08:30
My thighs are burning but I feel marvellous! I can't think of anything other than the physical exertion and taking in the wonderful landscape around me. I feel strong and out of breath, my heart pumping warm blood to my muscles. We're nearly at the top of the Coire Cas ridge.

10:00
The Cairngorm plateau is stunning. We have perfect visibility and can see for miles. Wow! Ben Macdui here we come.

The unbroken view of the snowy plateau extends for seven kilometres in front of us, our route to Scotland's second-highest mountain. Who knows, we may even get a view from the summit. I've never seen the plateau as clear as this.

12:00
There's no view from the summit of Ben Macdui. Oh, but it's good to be here. Steve takes a photo of me clad in full winter gear. I have a massive grin on my face.

15:47
There's a missed call on my phone. Who on earth is that?

16:45
Back in Aviemore at the Mountain Cafe, we each sit with a steaming cup of tea and an enormous slice of their famous cake. I suppose I'd better listen to my phone message.

'Hello Marisa, this is the breast care nurses. We've just had our MDT [multidisciplinary team meeting] and I'm afraid your histology results aren't back yet. We are going to cancel your appointment on Friday. They won't be ready for Monday either - we need to discuss in the MDT, which isn't until the afternoon.

Please can you ring to rearrange. There will be someone here until five-thirty.'

Oh shit! Shitty, shit shit shit! This isn't on! Not allowed! We cut our holiday short for these results. Aaarrghh!

16:55

I call the breast care nurses. A voice answers, 'Hello, breast care nurses?'

'Hello, this is Marisa Wray. I had a message to say that my results appointment for Friday is cancelled. We had to cut our holiday short to come in for the appointment. I'm feeling really upset.'

'I'm sorry. I know the waiting is horrible,' she sounds genuinely apologetic. 'We were hoping to discuss your results at our MDT today but they haven't been reported yet. I don't know why they offered you such an early appointment. Results are taking ten days or more to come through now.'

'Well, if they knew that why did they muck me around by offering me an appointment that was unlikely to happen? I could have enjoyed a full week's holiday.'

'All I can do is apologise. There's a backlog in the pathology department.'

'What sort of a backlog? Are they prioritising coronavirus tests above everything else?'

'I'm not sure. I think they're a pathologist down.'

'OK, so the message said that there wasn't any point in me attending on Monday either?'

'Trouble is that our MDT is in the afternoon and there are no appointments available after that on the Monday. And we don't know whether the results will be through by then anyway.'

This is really doing my head in. I am aware of my rising tone as I explain my dilemma. 'It would have been easy for me to attend on Friday, or even Monday as it's my working from home day, but after that it's going to cause me major stress. I already had to cancel one clinic when I spent all day in breast clinic. What's a doctor supposed to do! Work is going to be really busy next week

39

and the last thing I need is to be trying to juggle results appointments.'

'Let's see… well, how about one of us gives you a ring on Monday evening after the MDT?' she suggests, trying her best to be helpful. 'That way you'll know as much as we do. I promise, as soon as we know anything, you will too.'

'OK, thanks, I suppose that's the soonest you'll know anything. Sorry for being angry - I know it's not your fault. I'm just really stressed. OK, bye.'

I'm not sure what upsets me most: the fact we could have enjoyed our whole holiday had I been told the results would take longer to come through, or the fact the carpet's been pulled from under me and I'm going to be stewing for several more days. I'm more inclined to say it's the carpet. I can cope with most things if I have a plan, something to work towards. I can't stand it when the goal posts move or my careful plans are upended. To add insult to injury, they can't even tell me when the results might be ready.

We decide that staying on in the Cairngorms wouldn't feel right. I don't think I'd be able to relax or enjoy myself. Let's keep to the original plan and travel home tomorrow. There are lots of gardening jobs we can do on Friday.

19:00
My survival strategies kick in. I turn to the internet and start surfing cancer forums. I join the Cancer Research UK online forum, Cancer Chat. I feel this desperate need to reach out and find other people who are suffering too. My username is Spookcat. I love my cat!

19:20
I see a post on Cancer Chat under the thread 'Breast biopsy – waiting for my results'. Bingo! I introduce myself.

Hi,
I am in a similar position to you though am nearly 20 years older. I had 20 core biopsies taken last Thursday and was

40

supposed to go for my results appointment this Friday but they have postponed it indefinitely due to a backlog in the pathology dept. It's the waiting that is so hard.

I wish you the best possible results and peace of mind until then (as much as it is possible under the circumstances!).

Love Marisa (and Spook the cat)

22:42
There is a response to Spookcat.

Hi Marisa (and Spook the cat),
Welcome to the forum that nobody wants to join. I am so sorry that you are in this position.

You must be upset to have your results appointment postponed indefinitely. Waiting for results is one of the hardest times of our cancer journeys. Sadly, cancer is no respecter of age, but the very possibility that it could be cancer is terrifying.

I sincerely hope that you don't have too long to wait before you get your appointment. Can you bring someone with you to your appointment? This is always a good idea. I hope that your results are as good as they can be. We are always here for you in the meantime. Please keep in touch and let us know how you get on.

Kind regards

What a lovely reply. I feel a little heartened that someone at least understands how I'm feeling.

Thursday 5 March, 2020
10:00
I am at a service-station cafe. I call the patient experience team. No answer. I leave a message for them to call me back.

10.09
Someone calls back and offers for a colleague to call me later.

41

13:00

I am at another service-station cafe. My phone rings.

'Hello, is that Marisa?'

'Yes.'

'Is this a good time to talk? This is the patient experience team.'

'Yes, hello, it's fine.'

I explain how angry I am and how stressful I'm finding the whole experience. I know there's nothing they can do about it but I want to let someone know how it feels when your results appointment is cancelled.

The lady on the other end of the phone listens. I feel a little bit of relief.

15:00

I call the hospital switchboard. I'm sorely tempted to pretend to be the doctor asking for some results.

'Hello, could you put me through to the pathology lab please?'

On the third ring, I hear 'Hello, pathology?'

'Hello this is Doctor Wray. I normally have access to the path results, as I'm a doctor here, but I'm in a bit of a desperate situation. I was supposed to get my biopsy results tomorrow but my appointment was cancelled as they hadn't been reported yet. I'm resisting looking my own results up on the system and I know you can't read them out to me, but would you be able to tell me whether they've been reported or not? That would set my mind at rest a little.'

'OK, I'll look them up but I can't give you any details.' There is a brief pause, then 'Yes, they have been reported.'

'OK, thanks, at least that means they'll be discussed at the MDT on Monday. Thanks for your help.'

Friday 6 March, 2020
10:30

Gardening is not sufficient to take my mind off my results (or lack of them).

12:42
I turn to the Cancer Chat forum and start a new thread:

Is anyone else a doctor as well as a patient?

Hello! Are there any other doctors out there? I am awaiting
the histopathology report for my breast biopsy and am sorely
tempted to look up the results myself as I know they have
been reported but the MDT does not meet to discuss them
until Monday afternoon. I can't bear being in limbo. I don't
know when my follow-up appointment will be (was today
but got cancelled due to path lab backlog). I know the GMC
would frown upon it but do they really understand the
torture of being kept in the dark?

Oh, the dilemma of abusing your position as a doctor to ease your
own pain. In the UK it is heavily frowned upon to act as doctor
to your own friends or family, and even to yourself. We all do it
in minor ways, of course, but where do you draw the line? I didn't
hesitate to view my own mammogram on the radiology system I
use to view my patients' brain scans. I reasoned that the
radiographer had already showed it to me the day before and I
wasn't breaching anyone's trust. I was only trying to inform my
own research into what might be wrong with me. But accessing
my own pathology results before the doctor or the MDT had laid
eyes on them, that is something else. It feels wrong. Like an abuse
of my access to the system. I steel myself and think about probity
and being a good girl.
I manage to survive a weekend in limbo.

Chapter 4

We Don't Think It's Cancer

Monday 9 March, 2020
I'm lucky that my medical school job is both fascinating and absorbing. I spend the day mapping exam questions to learning objectives, which keeps my overactive brain from running away with itself on the cancer theme.

17:00
My phone rings. It's the breast care nurse. I'm on tenterhooks as she reads the pathology report to me.

'Area A shows atypical ductal hyperplasia (ADH) and area B shows flat epithelial atypia.' In non-medical speak, that means pre-cancerous changes to the linings of the breast ducts, which may or may not turn into cancer.

'So I haven't got cancer?'

'Apparently not,' she says, but goes on to tell me that in someone so young, they are not willing to let it go. 'The abnormal area is large and there might be something lurking in there that wasn't sampled. We'd like you to come back for a vacuum-assisted biopsy.'

Oh, right, so more waiting. 'Any idea when that will be?

'Within two weeks with any luck.'

17:30
I text my sister Jessica in New York.

> Hey Jessie, news is that there are pre-cancerous changes but nothing invasive. They did not get all the abnormal tissue so I need to have a bigger biopsy to rule out DCIS (ductal carcinoma in situ), a non-invasive cancer that can be cured with surgery. So cancer will not stop me coming to NY! Let's hope coronavirus doesn't stop me either!! Love you xxx

Thank God. Can't you just get them to take a big bit off anyway as a preventative measure?

17:38
I email my boss. (Wow, I'm super well organised!)

From: Wray Marisa
To: Alison
Subject: RE: Possible Breast Cancer

Hi Alison,

Just got my results through. Histology shows atypical hyperplasia so they want to do a vacuum biopsy to check for DCIS. Not sure when it will be yet but I might need to take a day or two off this week or next. At least it's not invasive ductal carcinoma, which is what I was fearing.

Thank you for being so supportive. The waiting is horrible!

BW
Marisa

20:44
I am back on Cancer Chat.

Breast biopsy - waiting for my results.

Hi everyone on this thread (do replies go to all or just to the person you reply to?)
Finally got results today. I have atypical ductal hyperplasia which I understand is pre-cancerous cell changes. I now need a vacuum biopsy to check the whole area for DCIS. I am very relieved that it isn't invasive, so at worst I will need wide local excision, at best yearly monitoring. So good news on the whole!

My gosh I feel exhausted with all the waiting and anticipation though!
Thanks for being here ladies.
Xxx

Tuesday 10 March, 2020
Today is my Uni day (the one day a week when I work for Lancaster University Medical School), so I'm puffing up the hill to the station on my Brompton bike. I fold it up on the train and reassemble it at the other end for the twenty-five-minute ride along the canal path to campus. Unknown to me, this is the last time I will be making this journey in 2020. From next week onwards, all university staff will have to work from home and soon, all student placements will be suspended.

11:32
I email my team leader and secretaries.

Just an update.

My worst fears have been allayed as the biopsy only showed pre-cancerous cells, not invasive cancer. I still need to go for a vacuum biopsy where they suck out a larger area to check they haven't missed anything more cancerous. But it looks as though the worst-case scenario would be a small operation. I am waiting for the vacuum-biopsy appointment to come through but it's likely to be this week or next.

This means I may have to take time off at short notice as I will take whatever appointment they offer me.

The whole experience has been very traumatic! I may not be fully functional as the psychological stress has been immense, not least because Steve took the whole thing very hard too.

I will be in tomorrow unless they call me in for biopsy sooner!

BW
Marisa

Even though it's my uni day, I still have to think about my clinical job and make sure the right hand knows what the left hand is doing.

Wednesday 11 March, 2020
It feels strange being back in clinic after my holiday. I feel drained from all the waiting, though relieved I don't have cancer. I start to wonder whether I was premature in informing work colleagues as it's likely to amount to nothing. That day at breast clinic had me convinced that I had cancer. Hey ho. I'm sure they will just put me on yearly surveillance now.

I do a bit of googling on ADH. OK, so I'm at work, but this is all part of my CPD - continuing professional development (we have to do fifty hours a year to keep in good faith with the Royal College of Psychiatrists!). Fascinating stuff. Some people even argue about where ADH ends and DCIS begins. I'm so glad I'm not a histopathologist. I never got on too well with looking at pink-stained cells down a microscope. It gave me eye ache and I couldn't tell one type of morphology from another. ADH can grow in all sorts of funny shapes and you have to have a practiced eye to differentiate it from low-grade DCIS. ADH is not cancer. DCIS is cancer: ductal carcinoma in situ - cancer in the ducts that hasn't yet broken out of the duct wall into the surrounding tissue. Apparently if you have multifocal, calcified ADH then your chances of developing invasive breast cancer are about fifty percent over twenty-five years (Kader et al. 2018). So that's why they'll want to keep an eye on me.

The other thing I was never any good at was probability. I never could quite get my head around relative risk and odds ratio. However, one thing I do understand is the absolute risk. Before my nipple started bleeding, my absolute risk of having breast cancer was about two percent (this is the approximate population risk for women aged forty-six). How do you translate a background absolute risk of two percent into a fifty percent risk

47

that my ADH cells will develop into cancer sometime in the next twenty-five years? I decide not to think about it.

Thursday 12 March, 2020
I'm at work pretending everything is normal. There's a whole lot of people in the big meeting room. They're all smiley and friendly looking, and I see some members of our team beaming from ear to ear and jumping up and down excitedly. I'm in a helpful mood today, so in I go and introduce myself.

It's a team from the Trust doing a quality visit, and some of my colleagues have been giving a presentation. The visiting team is keen to find out how we do things, so I gleefully offer to take one of them with me this morning, as long as the patients agree, that is.

One of the privileges of being an old age psychiatrist in the community is that we are still permitted to visit our patients at home if they are unable to make it to clinic. I love home visits. You learn so much more about a person, and it's also much easier to remember them!

It all goes marvellously, and my companion is delighted to see how well we work together as a team. I get a buzz from this kind of thing.

In my afternoon clinic, I have a patient who absolutely doesn't want to know they have Alzheimer's disease (this is unusual - most people do want to know) but does want to take the tablets that help your memory. Next, I empathise with their spouse over how hard it must be to assume the carer role. Sometimes just acknowledging it helps.

My final patient of the day has three mental health diagnoses, not just one. I have recently diagnosed dementia in addition to the pre-existing conditions, and the family have to hold their noses because the patient keeps forgetting to wash.

I am unaware that this is my last normal day at work. The very next day, Friday 13 March, we are instructed to only see a patient if it is both essential and necessary. We are about to enter the strange new world of the coronavirus.

19:44
I send a message via WhatsApp to my sister Laura in Milan.

Hey Lalsie, Steve wants to know what you think about Boris sacrificing lives for the sake of the UK economy? Xxx

All I can say is try and stay home as much as possible or up a mountain on your own!! Try not to go to public places like cafes and things... what Boris should be doing is suggesting all this to people but he's too scared of losing Tory voters who want to go and see the horse racing.

Yup, our thoughts too. He says we are 4 weeks behind Italy but we think it's more like 2 weeks.

Yup 2 weeks. Also for NY at this rate hopefully they will reimburse your flight - by 31 March Trump will have extended the travel ban to the UK too.

Ah, there goes my trip to see my sister in New York. She lives a mile away from the epicentre of the virus. We all watch with horror as the deaths from COVID-19 in northern Italy rise exponentially.

Chapter 5

Brave New COVID-19 World

Friday 20 March, 2020
07:00
I have the most horrendous headache. Well, it's not quite as bad as it was last night but I didn't sleep well at all. I'm sure it's because I didn't finish work until gone seven last night as my colleague and I were trying to get through a mammoth number of dementia diagnoses. I normally do my dementia diagnoses on a Friday but I was allowing my guilt complex to force me to squeeze Friday's work into Thursday evening. I've been spending rather too much time glued to my screen, keeping up with the latest COVID-19 news and attending webinars on topics such as how to explain to a patient that they would be unlikely to survive being ventilated in intensive care. I also find it really stressful not being able to see patients face to face; I feel as though I'm making decisions blindfolded.

09:30
This time Steve is coming with me to breast clinic. We have to sanitise our hands when we arrive then I grab us each a sneaky coffee at the staff restaurant because we're early. The clinic is dead quiet compared to last time and I don't have to wait long before I'm called in. Steve might as well go out for a walk because 'I may be some time'.

10:30
There's a very chatty radiologist with a lovely Irish accent carrying out my procedure today. He's refreshingly frank and is the first person to level with me on what he thinks the diagnosis is likely to be. About 20 percent of core biopsies miss a cancer, and he thinks it highly likely that I have DCIS. When you've been a doctor for long enough you begin to recognise recurring

patterns. Just as I look at a brain scan and say 'Alzheimer's', he looked at my mammogram and said 'DCIS'.

I quiz him about ductal carcinoma in situ. It ranges from low (most like normal cells) to high grade (least like normal cells and most likely to become invasive cancer), and in some cases never does anything other than sit there. However, you can't just leave it in case it does transform into invasive disease, which will generally happen eventually, but who knows when? OK, so if I do have DCIS, what then?

'That's up to the surgeon,' he says. 'Sometimes if it's low-grade it's just watchful waiting.'

11:00

I already know the drill on the stereotactically guided biopsy mammogram machine. I'm going to be lying on this trolley for some time so I try to arrange myself as comfortably as possible. It's actually not too bad. I call it a trolley for want of a better word but it's a fully-reclining padded chair, a bit like they have at the dentist. Nurses are bustling about the room getting equipment ready and checking if I'm comfortable. It's all quite cheery.

'OK, we're going to position you on the machine.'

I wriggle into place, lying on my right side so that my left boob is splatted side-on onto the landing pad. Then the breast flattener comes down.

'OK, move forward a little so all of your breast tissue is on the slab.'

Mmm, very comfy.

'We're going to put some local anaesthetic in now.'

Ouch! That stings.

A minute later, 'Can you feel this?'

'Er, yes a bit. Can I have some more local?' OK, I'm completely numb now.

They are sampling from two areas. One is quite deep in the breast, the other very near the nipple. I have to sign a disclaimer to say I understand there is a risk of injury to my skin around the nipple. I tell the radiologist that I have faith in his skills. He says once the VAB (vacuum-assisted biopsy) machine starts, it can have a bit of a mind of its own and you can't stop it from completing its mission and sucking up all the tissue it wants to. It can be difficult to gauge exactly how close to the skin it can go without sucking a bit of skin in with the breast tissue. Oh, great!

Close shave. My skin is still intact but only just. Clever radiologist... phew!

One of the adverse events I was warned about on the disclaimer was the risk of haemorrhage (bleeding). I take sertraline, a selective serotonin transporter reuptake inhibitor antidepressant. I am lucky that on the whole, as long as I take my antidepressants, my mental health remains relatively stable. Stop them and I plunge into a black hole every time. One of the side effects of SSRIs is that they make you more likely to bruise or bleed.

'Well, I never!' says the radiologist after I regale him with a little lecture on how my antidepressant stops my blood from clotting.

'The effect is a bit similar to taking aspirin,' I explain.

12:00

I am being looked after by a very attentive nurse who is solicitous about my wellbeing. She is concerned because the two little holes in my breast won't stop bleeding. My defender and chaperone growls at the other nurses who are getting antsy because they need to move on to the next case, and I'm hogging the high-tech room where their only stereotaxy machine is housed.

'I'm not fussed,' I say. 'Here, I'll exert pressure on it while you wheel me into another room so you can get on with your work in here.'

My companion and I sit (well, I'm still lying down actually) in an empty clinic room and talk about inconsequential things.

12:45

My holes have finally stopped bleeding. The nurse seals them with steristrips then covers the lot with a giant bandage. Why do bandages have to be so big! I think they're designed to cause maximum inconvenience in the shower. I'm not allowed to get the wounds wet nor remove the dressing for three days.

The radiologist pops back in to arrange a results appointment. They usually do it over the phone if it's straightforward but face to face if it's complex or needs further treatment.

'Can I have it over the phone? It's just that having to cancel clinics to come here is a pain.' I'm given a telephone appointment for Tuesday 31 March. 'The results will definitely be reported by then, yeah?' I don't want a repeat of what happened with my last results appointment.

13:00
Steve and I walk into town for some lunch. I explain to him that it's probably DCIS and that I might need a lumpectomy if I'm unlucky. We'll see. They might still decide to sit on it and keep an eye on me.

Unlike last time, I feel no qualms whatsoever about taking the whole day off work. The patient instructions tell you to rest for twenty-four hours after the VAB, so I'm being a good patient and not a stressed doctor for a change.

Steve and I have both been having a rough time of it lately. He handed in his notice at work nearly three months ago and is not feeling on top of the world, to put it mildly. He has never faced unemployment before, nor taken more than one day off sick in his whole working life. It began with someone defacing a photo of him on the work notice board by sticking a drawing pin in his eye. He reported the incident to the then Chief Executive, but the dysfunctional management style continued. By the time he quit he was so worn down he could not even contemplate taking them to court. It makes me angry just to think about it. He says he doesn't know himself anymore. He has been suffering from existential angst for a while now and this new health issue of mine has dealt him a severe blow. I'm torn between wanting to lean on him for support and wanting to shield him from the horrors going on in my mind.

18:00

I'm back home. I'm not feeling brilliant but I need some fresh air. I head out for the Helm, our nearest little hill, which overlooks our village and Kendal.

18:37

I receive a text from Louise, a nurse colleague and friend.

Hi Marisa, how did it go? Hope all went well and you're not too sore xxx

All fine. Bit sore and it took ages. Results in 10 days. How're things at work? Xxx

Oh dear you poor thing at least it's over, take care & rest up, hope you stocked up on wine! Work's as ok as it can be given the current situation! Keeping us super busy, the force is strong ☺ see you Wednesday. xx

Steve very down about job situation. Not sure how to support him while preserving my own mental health... God help me! Am walking along top of Helm. Had to get out. xxx

Oh no, in the dark? I'm still at work, which way are you heading? Do you want me to meet you? Fancy a drink? Xxx

Quite light still. Told Steve I wouldn't be long but how about a cup of tea at work then can u drop me home?

Sure hun, are you walking here or do you want me to meet you? X

Louise is a lifesaver! One cup of tea and a chat later, I feel less of a wreck.

20:30

I feel really worn out. I'm going to have an early night reading in bed. The local anaesthetic has worn off and my boob is sore. I can't lie on my left side. I've also got a sore throat and my cervical lymph nodes (glands in your neck which come up when you have a cold or any respiratory infection) are swollen and sore. Paracetamol helps a bit.

Saturday 21 March, 2020
08:00

I'm ill. I feel like I've got a virus or something. Not stay-in-bed ill but I'm not right.

'You need to get a Covid test,' Steve tells me, sounding mildly alarmed.

'Er, I doubt it's Covid, I haven't got a temperature or a cough.'

'Not yet, but those symptoms might take a day or two to develop. You work for the NHS [National Health Service] for crying out loud, you should be able to get a test.'

I feel like I'm moving through treacle. 'OK, let me turn my work phone on.'

08:30

I call the hospital switchboard.

'Hello, can you put me through to the Covid-testing centre please?'

'Er, that's not run by the hospital.'

'Oh, right. Do you know where the test centre is? Or how to get tested? I'm a doctor and have symptoms and just want to get tested but with it being the weekend I don't know where to start.'

'Oh, you poor thing. I think if you go through occupational health they can arrange a test for you.'

'Do you know where the test centre is?'

'It's somewhere near the hospital but I'm not sure where.'

'OK, thanks.'

08:35

I call the Trust Covid hotline. There's a recorded message:

'Hello, this line is open from nine to five. Please call within those hours. If you have a fever and a new persistent cough, please call NHS111.'

Oh great!

Steve calls out, 'Have you got through to anyone?'

'I'm trying but no one's open until nine and the hospital says they don't run the Covid-testing centre and don't know where it is.'

'You'd have thought the NHS would be able to test its own staff! You have to get a test, it's ridiculous!'

09:01

I try the Trust Covid hotline again.

'Hello?' answers a colleague.

'Is this the right number to call if I've got possible Covid symptoms? I feel flu-like with lethargy, achy limbs, headache, aching eyes and sore throat. No fever or cough though.'

'OK, you'd better start self-isolating then. The current guidance is for seven days, so that takes us up to next Saturday, twenty-eighth of March. You don't need to take sick leave if you're self-isolating for possible Covid symptoms. I'll sort it out on the HR system for you.'

'Thanks. Erm, I'm supposed to be on annual leave on Thursday and Friday next week. I shouldn't need to forfeit that should I?'

'No, that's right. I'll cancel that leave for you.'

'Thank you. Um, do you know if there's anywhere I can go to get tested?'

'We don't have our own test centres yet so we're relying on NHS111. I think some colleagues have had some success by going via occupational health at the main hospital, though.'

'Ah, right. Thanks, I'll try that.' I feel grateful for her help.

09:15

I call occupational health.

'Hello, I'm a doctor working for the Trust and I was told that you're organising Covid tests for people who are symptomatic?'

'Do you have a fever and a new persistent cough?'

'Well, no, but I've got other symptoms and want to get tested. My husband is very upset about the situation and is insisting I get tested. Is there no way I can get a test?'

'I'm sorry but you don't meet the criteria. Bye.'

09:30

Right, I'm getting in the car and driving to the hospital to try to find the test centre. Maybe if I just turn up they won't turn me away. I feel so desperate. Steve is beside himself with worry over the lack of testing. There's so little information and we feel so powerless. I think the stress of the last few weeks has got to us both. We don't normally react like this when one of us is a bit ill.

10:10

I'm driving round and round the hospital grounds trying to find the test centre. There are no signs to it anywhere. I feel like such an idiot. Did I think I could just turn up and get tested? I call occupational health again.

'Hello, I called earlier and was told that I didn't meet the criteria for a test, but I have a bit of a cough now, ahem ahem.'

'Is it a persistent cough?'

'Well, it's getting more persistent.'

'How long have you had it?'

'Since this morning.'

'I'm sorry but you don't fulfil the criteria for a test.'

'But I'm a doctor working in a hospital and I need a test. My husband won't let me back in the house until I've been tested! I don't know what to do, I can't go back home! I've been driving round the hospital car park trying to find the test centre. Please, can you just help me?'

I start to sob down the phone.

'Look,' the voice is gentler. 'I'm sorry you're feeling so upset but we can't help. Does your husband need help?

'Hic, no, it's OK, I'm sorry I know it's not your fault. I'll just try and calm down a bit.'

10:15

I call Steve.

'Hi Love, I've been driving around and I can't get tested. I've called numerous numbers and all I get told is I don't meet the criteria. I can't even find where the test centre is. I'm feeling so desperate! I even told them that you wouldn't let me back in the house until I got tested and they still said no!' I burst into tears again.

'Lovey, don't worry, at least you tried. Come home and get some rest.'

'OK, I'll just park up for a bit and when I feel safe enough to drive, I'll head back.'

I spend the afternoon painting watercolour, which soothes me a little. I also call a friend to tell her the saga. She makes just the right noises over the phone and empathises with how stressful it must be for Steve.

14:40

I receive a text from Mum.

How r u feeling?

I'm fine. Just tired, sore throat and headache.

Gargle with boiled salted water, suck Strepsils & step up vit C & zinc. And rest. All helped me. Keep us in loop. How is Steve?

20:50

I have a message on WhatsApp from my sister Laura in Milan.

Misie how are you feeling?

Just like I've got a nasty cold. No fever or cough. Aches and pains, headache and sore throat. Probably is just a cold but no way to tell... how are you all? xxx

Argh that's annoying, but glad you don't have any other symptoms. Who knows what it is, will you manage to have time off work to recover properly?

Yes am self-isolating.

That's good, just make sure you look after yourself as I think the worst thing is trying to carry on (like we all would usually do if we just had a bad cold!!). And follow Mum's very helpful advice lol.

Yup. Steve is going to drop chocolates and card off at his mum's tomorrow so will have a bit of time to myself. He is in such a bad way. I don't know how to help him feel better.

Oh dear, I'm sorry to hear that. I hope you do manage to have a break - you just need to sit on the sofa under a blanket and watch telly!! I sent Mum flowers for tomorrow but no idea if they will actually get delivered!! Hopefully they will without risking anyone having to breach social distancing!!

Tomorrow is Mothering Sunday. I find it one of the hardest days of the year as I can't have children and it feels like this day is rubbing salt in the wound. If there were two things I could change about my life, it would be my depressive illness and my childlessness. If I could change only one thing, it would be the childlessness. And yes, I've heard it all before: 'It will happen if you just stop trying so hard' (I'm too old now anyway – my ovaries gave up long ago) and 'I know someone who built her family with donor eggs.' Ever ask how much it cost or meet anyone who tried over and over again with donor eggs but their uterus was just not an environment where a baby wanted to grow? Oh, and 'How about that actress who finally got pregnant after twelve cycles of IVF!' We tried IVF and the emotional impact of failure had me on my knees after just two cycles. I take my hat off to anyone who managed twelve! 'Why don't you just adopt?' Well, try convincing social services that you will cope with adopting if you have a recurrent depressive illness. I also defy anyone to go through the process of applying to adopt. We did and it broke my heart. I just couldn't do it. Neither Steve nor I had the emotional strength to cope.

I try to focus on spoiling my own mother and Steve's mum, but in truth it's a bit of a relief that I'm going to be spending Mother's Day at home on my own. I don't have to endure families in restaurants making a fuss of their mother, while I feel barren and 'other'. I have managed to send my mum a brilliant card featuring Wonder Woman. All the Mother's Day cards in the shops were horrid but I found this one in the children's birthday card aisle. Yay! Strictly speaking Steve shouldn't go and see his mum either but if he doesn't go, the psychological effect on her will be devastating. She's in her eighties and lives alone, just over an hour away. He will make sure he stays in the garden at least two metres away from her at all times. He explains to her that I have to stay at home to self-isolate.

Sunday 22 March, 2020
Steve's mum appreciates his visit and the weather is beautiful so he is able to remain in the garden. He returns exhausted but glad to have been able to see her. I've been a couch potato all day and am all the better for it. Victoria wishes me happy Mothers day on WhatsApp. I'm over the moon! The term "stepmother" has been banned in our house since Steve and I met when Victoria was 11. I can't wipe the smile off my face.

Monday 23 March, 2020
09:15
I'm feeling a little better today. I have a sneaky peek under the dressing on my breast. The wounds look more or less sealed. It should be OK to take the big bandage off, shower then put some micropore tape and gauze over the steristrips. There's much less bruising than last time too. I think back gratefully to the nurse who made it her mission not to let me bruise. I now have an arc of five very neat holes on the left side of my left breast.

This virus feels like nothing I've ever had before. Normally when I have a cold I have a blocked nose, but my nose is clear. I have no fever and my cough is a bit productive rather than dry. Who knows whether it's Covid or not? The headache has subsided a bit, so has the sore throat, but I have this aching feeling deep behind my eyes as if they are sunken in. And I feel so lethargic and lacking in energy. I can't be bothered to even leave the house (good thing, as I'm not allowed to). Then again, if it was Covid, wouldn't I be much sicker? People I know who've tested positive have been bedridden for several days at least. Maybe it's just a winter bug of some sort.

11:49
I email my team leader and secretaries.

From: Wray Marisa
To: admin mailbox
Subject: Self-isolating

Hi all,

I think you probably already know from HR but I am self-isolating. Started symptoms on Saturday. No fever but have lethargy, headache, eye ache and sore throat. Chest feels a bit tight this morning with a bit of a cough. It's probably not Covid but who knows?

I don't feel ill enough to stay in bed so will do whatever I can from home. That said, trying to get my work computer to do anything is proving a challenge. I think the server is still overwhelmed by remote workers.

BW
Marisa

The weather is beautiful. It's sunny and warm. I sit in the garden through the afternoon. My third-year medical students have all

61

been sent home but they have given me a whole lot of cases to mark. It keeps me busy.

I'm also following COVID-19 stats and making my own spreadsheet. According to *The Guardian* newspaper, 83,945 people in the UK have been tested for COVID-19: 77,295 are negative, 6,650 are positive. The death toll so far is 335. Having a sister in Milan, where they have been in strict lockdown for two weeks already, brings it into sharp focus. Lal is confined to her apartment with her husband Mario and their daughters who are one and almost four. I don't envy her! The curve of rising infections in the UK looks alarmingly like that of Italy if you superimpose the graphs. We're just a couple of weeks behind and infection rates are not showing any sign of slowing down.

20:30
There is a public announcement by Prime Minister Boris Johnson.

'Good evening,

The coronavirus is the biggest threat this country has faced for decades – and this country is not alone.
All over the world we are seeing the devastating impact of this invisible killer.
And so tonight I want to update you on the latest steps we are taking to fight the disease and what you can do to help.
And I want to begin by reminding you why the UK has been taking the approach that we have.
Without a huge national effort to halt the growth of this virus, there will come a moment when no health service in the world could possibly cope; because there won't be enough ventilators, enough intensive care beds, enough doctors and nurses.
And as we have seen elsewhere, in other countries that also have fantastic healthcare systems, that is the moment of real danger.
To put it simply, if too many people become seriously unwell at one time, the NHS will be unable to handle it - meaning

more people are likely to die, not just from coronavirus but from other illnesses as well.

So it's vital to slow the spread of the disease.

Because that is the way we reduce the number of people needing hospital treatment at any one time, so we can protect the NHS's ability to cope - and save more lives.

And that's why we have been asking people to stay at home during this pandemic.

And though huge numbers are complying - and I thank you all - the time has now come for us all to do more.

From this evening I must give the British people a very simple instruction - you must stay at home.

Because the critical thing we must do is stop the disease spreading between households.

That is why people will only be allowed to leave their home for the following very limited purposes:

- shopping for basic necessities, as infrequently as possible;
- one form of exercise a day - for example a run, walk, or cycle - alone or with members of your household;
- any medical need, to provide care or to help a vulnerable person; and
- travelling to and from work, but only where this is absolutely necessary and cannot be done from home.

That's all - these are the only reasons you should leave your home.

You should not be meeting friends. If your friends ask you to meet, you should say no.

You should not be meeting family members who do not live in your home.

You should not be going shopping except for essentials like food and medicine - and you should do this as little as you can. And use food delivery services where you can.

If you don't follow the rules, the police will have the powers to enforce them, including through fines and dispersing gatherings.

To ensure compliance with the Government's instruction to stay at home, we will immediately:

- close all shops selling non-essential goods, including clothing and electronic stores and other premises including libraries, playgrounds and outdoor gyms, and places of worship;
- we will stop all gatherings of more than two people in public - excluding people you live with; and
- we'll stop all social events, including weddings, baptisms and other ceremonies, but excluding funerals.

Parks will remain open for exercise but gatherings will be dispersed.

No prime minister wants to enact measures like this.

I know the damage that this disruption is doing and will do to people's lives, to their businesses and to their jobs.

And that's why we have produced a huge and unprecedented programme of support both for workers and for business.

And I can assure you that we will keep these restrictions under constant review. We will look again in three weeks and relax them if the evidence shows we are able to.

But at present there are just no easy options. The way ahead is hard, and it is still true that many lives will sadly be lost.

And yet it is also true that there is a clear way through.

Day by day we are strengthening our amazing NHS with 7,500 former clinicians now coming back to the service.

With the time you buy - by simply staying at home - we are increasing our stocks of equipment.

We are accelerating our search for treatments.

We are pioneering work on a vaccine.

And we are buying millions of testing kits that will enable us to turn the tide on this invisible killer.

I want to thank everyone who is working flat out to beat the virus.

Everyone from the supermarket staff to the transport workers to the carers to the nurses and doctors on the frontline.

But in this fight we can be in no doubt that each and every one of us is directly enlisted.

Each and every one of us is now obliged to join together.

To halt the spread of this disease.
To protect our NHS and to save many many thousands of lives.
And I know that as they have in the past so many times.
The people of this country will rise to that challenge.
And we will come through it stronger than ever.
We will beat the coronavirus and we will beat it together.
And therefore, I urge you at this moment of national emergency to stay at home, protect our NHS and save lives.

Thank you.'

And so the UK lockdown begins.

Tuesday 24 March, 2020
Steve and I are both working from home. Steve's job finishes at the end of this week. He's feeling stressed about it to say the least. How is he going to get another job in the current circumstances? We were supposed to be going to Keswick for a couple of nights at the end of the week as a birthday treat for me, but of course we've had to cancel. At least we'll get our money back.

I read an article in an Italian newspaper about why Italy has such a high death rate from COVID-19. Will the NHS be overwhelmed with people needing intensive care and ventilation, as happened in northern Italy? I'm not even thinking about my biopsy results.

13:14
I receive an email from my consultant colleague who is also self-isolating with mild symptoms (she can't get tested either!). She's in shock because she's just found out that she was in a meeting last week with a colleague who has tested Covid-positive. Everyone else who attended that meeting also has symptoms. I send an email in reply.

From: Wray Marisa
To:Deepa
Subject: RE: Cancel virtual clinic today

Hi,

Oh no, hope your symptoms don't get any worse. Take care
of yourself and family. I will get in touch with team
tomorrow. If you're feeling well enough, we can still
WhatsApp group tomorrow?

BW
Marisa

The four consultants who cover our catchment area have shared
our personal mobile numbers and formed a WhatsApp group so
we can communicate with each other from home or wherever we
happen to be. Thank God for technology!

Wednesday 25 March, 2020
10:00
Bummer, I can't get my computer to do anything on the work
server. This is hopeless. What's a self-isolating gal supposed to do?
There's nothing else for it. I'm going to have to go to the hospital
and work in the car park. I should be able to get a signal there. I'm
feeling a lot better - well enough to cycle up there, in fact. It's a
beautiful day.

10:30
I'm in the hospital car park sitting on a stone with my computer
on my knee. A physician colleague spots me and comes to ask if I
need help. I warn her to keep her distance as I have mild
symptoms.
    'Can I at least bring you a chair?' she asks.
    I gratefully accept her offer, along with a glass of water. I make
sure I keep my distance at all times and get my secretary to pass
me some disinfectant wipes through my office window so I can

disinfect the chair. Whoever heard of a consultant working from the hospital car park because she couldn't get her computer to work from home? Desperate times deserve desperate measures. I know I'm not supposed to be here but the other consultant is off sick and there is work to be done. I'm not going near anybody and at least I'm outside. I don't even know if I've got the dreaded virus, for goodness' sake!

I'm running a 'virtual clinic' with Louise, a specialist nurse colleague and expert in dementia. The doctor no longer sees every patient for a dementia diagnosis. The nurses visit the patient to hear their history, collect collateral information and do a memory test. The patient also has a brain scan. Making a diagnosis is like putting a jigsaw puzzle together. If we have enough information, we can fit the pieces together and see the whole picture. It means we can make dementia diagnoses efficiently. I normally manage to go through three or four cases per hour in this way. So, armed with Louise's information, my diagnostic acumen and the brain-scan viewing system on my laptop, we try to run the 'virtual clinic'.

How farcical. Louise is sitting in my office and I am outside in the car park about two metres away from her, facing the other way. My computer audio won't work so I have to speak to Louise on my mobile phone while looking up patients on the computer. I'm glad that I've brought my hat because the sun is beating mercilessly down on my head. No shade here. It's hard to see my computer screen in the glare but I'll have to manage. I'm beginning to feel a bit stressed! I dictate a letter for each patient and manage to dock the Dictaphone (which Louise passed to me through the window) to a satisfying 'copying jobs from dictation device' confirmatory message. By the time Louise and I have gone through seven cases, my brain is addled and I have a monumental headache. I don't feel quite as well as I felt earlier. Time to go home.

17:00
Heck, I'm exhausted. I think I'll work from home tomorrow and Friday. I am supposed to be self-isolating after all.

Saturday 28 March, 2020
I am officially allowed to go out. Steve and I decide to use our one permitted form of exercise to explore some of the local area on foot. We discover fields full of lambs and a graveyard full of daffodils. There are places on our doorstep we didn't even know were there. My spirits are revived!

Monday 30 March, 2020
Today is my birthday. I always try to take the day off on my birthday to do nice things. I attempt to go for a run over the Helm. I haven't been for the two weeks I have been ill. My lungs feel as if they are about to explode and I keep coughing uncontrollably. Oh my, this is hard!

Tuesday 31 March, 2020
16:00
They're supposed to have phoned me with my results by now. Probably just running late. Stay calm.

16:30
Running very late.

17:00
Still no phone call.

17:30
Now I'm feeling really agitated.
    Steve and I go for a walk down to the river. We go this way whenever we need to get some head space, stretch our legs or walk the cat - Spook has always followed us on this route because it's not too far from home.
    'It's just common courtesy to let your patients know if you're not going to be able to call them!' By now I am jumping up and down a bit. 'I would never just ignore a patient and not let them know that either I was late or I needed to reschedule our appointment. Two hours late! They're not going to call me now are they - I'm sure they finish at five. So rude!'

'Maybe it's like last time and the results aren't through yet?' Steve suggests reasonably.

'Well at least last time they had the decency to call me to tell me that!'

I'm in a state of great indignation but deep down there's also a little niggle. The radiologist did say they only give results over the phone if they are straight forward. This doesn't bode well...

Wednesday 1 April, 2020

I'm at work. In body if not in mind. Somehow, I manage to make a very constructive contribution to a meeting about extended working due to COVID-19.

The Trust has issued an edict that senior doctors must work at weekends over and above what we already provide on call. A consultant must be present in the hospital over the weekend until further notice, and we have to sort out between us how we are going to cover it.

Luckily, I have a new colleague who is very helpful and together we propose a way to cover weekends which causes the least amount of pain to everyone involved. The main aim is to prevent the NHS from becoming overwhelmed and to keep psychiatric patients from being admitted via the Emergency Department.

12:30

I have a missed call and a voicemail asking me to ring the hospital appointments line. Hurray! They tell me that I do have an appointment to see the surgeon - at ten on Friday morning - it's just that no one thought to inform me of it sooner.

15:42

I send an email to my line manager and consultant colleague.

From: Wray Marisa
To: Alison and Deepa
Subject: Breast clinic on Friday

Hi both, I've been asked to attend a face-to-face appointment at breast clinic at 10:00 on Friday 3rd April. Just wanted to let you know. I was supposed to get my results over the phone yesterday but only heard this morning that they want to see me. I am sorely tempted to look up my own histology, as I am still in the dark. Radiologist told me that they usually only give results face to face if they need to discuss further treatment. So it probably means they want to discuss the risks of operating or whatever treatment I might need. I had hoped to avoid anything like this but hey ho.

I will keep you posted.

BW
Marisa

17:26

From: Alison
To: Wray Marisa
Subject: RE: Breast clinic on Friday

I have fingers and toes crossed that all goes well on Friday Marisa.

And on a separate note entirely, thank you so much for such constructive and helpful contribution around weekend working today - massively appreciated!

A

Thursday 2 April, 2020
I am so grateful to my secretary for giving me a light diary today. To say that I am not firing on all four cylinders would be an understatement. I busy myself at work by crunching data on our team's performance. It gives me a sense of accomplishment, at least. I wonder whether I'll sleep tonight?

Chapter 6

DCIS

Friday 3 April, 2020
10:00
Steve and I are sitting in the surgeon's office. It's very sparse. Maybe they've had to remove anything on which COVID-19 might breed. There's a nurse there, too. The surgeon apologises for us having to sit so far away and asks whether we want him to wear a mask. We tell him no, it's fine.

'What do you understand from your investigations so far?' he asks me.

'I went to breast clinic on a two-week wait as I had nipple discharge and my mammogram showed multiple segmental pleiomorphic calcifications. The core biopsies were equivocal as they only showed atypical ductal hyperplasia and, what is it? Flat epithelial atypia? So they wanted to do vacuum biopsies to rule out DCIS. The radiologist told me that it was likely that I had DCIS.'

'That's right,' he confirms. 'The histology report from the vacuum biopsy shows two areas that look like low-grade DCIS.'

'Okay.'

'What do you know about treatment of DCIS?'

'I think it's surgical, isn't it?'

'Yes. Now, because the abnormal area takes up a large proportion of your breast, the required treatment is a mastectomy.'

Silence. I'm in shock. This certainly wasn't what I was expecting to hear.

Steve steps in, trying to keep calm. 'I know I'm not medical but it seems ridiculous to me that in the 21st century we have to resort to butchery! Is that really the only option? Surely there are other alternatives? There are cancer breakthroughs all the time. Isn't there a medication she can take? One of the new ones?'

I know he's thinking of a friend of ours who has just started on a newly approved cancer treatment.

'There is no medication for DCIS,' the surgeon explains. 'Because DCIS isn't an invasive cancer it doesn't respond to medication. The trouble is that it can become invasive, but we have no way of predicting when. The only way to make sure it doesn't is to cut it out and make sure we get all of it.'

'Isn't there a trial she can go on or something?' Steve asks.

'There is a trial which we're participating in where we leave the DCIS and just monitor yearly to see if it transforms into invasive disease.' The surgeon looks directly at me. 'The trouble is that due to your age and the extent of the abnormal area, you're not eligible.'

'Do you have to take her whole breast?' Steve tries.

'We need to get clear margins so if I only did a lumpectomy the remaining breast would look very deformed. A mastectomy with a reconstruction would give a better result.'

'Love, the trouble is that my breasts are small. Once they've cut the abnormal area out there won't be much left!' I turn to the surgeon. 'Can I have an implant? Would that be the best? I don't really know anything about the other types of reconstruction.'

'We do the pre-pectoral type of implant. We were one of the first centres to start doing it. I think that would be best for you. But you need to go away and read about the different options and think it over. The recovery periods are quite different. For an immediate implant reconstruction, you're looking six to eight weeks. For reconstruction using your own muscles or fat, it's more like ten to twelve weeks at least.'

'So the implant can be done at the same time as the mastectomy?'

'Yes. But we're not operating at all at the moment. You do understand? It's just not safe. I've seen colleagues in ICU with Covid. You don't want to be in hospital right now - you don't want to put yourself at risk. The type of breast cancer you have is the best one to have, if you see what I mean. It could be years before it does anything that might put your life at risk.'

'How long am I likely to be waiting? It's just that it won't go down well with work if I announce that I have breast cancer and will need eight weeks of sick leave but I have no idea when it will be. Are we talking next year? In the autumn?'

'No, not next year. It could be the autumn though. What we're doing is reviewing patients in your situation after three months.'

'So, you'll see me in three-months' time?' I ask in disbelief.

'The breast care nurse will give you a booklet which you can read through. The nurses are available for you to phone whenever you need to.'

'Right. So I just carry on as normal until I see you again in three months.' And forget all about the cancer in my breast that could attack at any moment.

The surgeon just gives me an apologetic look.

We are ushered by the nurse into another room, a veritable repository for leaflets and booklets. She can tell we are both in shock. We stand around like a pair of lemons.

'It's not the news you wanted to hear but you're in the best hands, you know,' she says to reassure us.

'Thank you. Strange times, these, aren't they? Are you seeing many patients face to face?'

'Very few. In fact, today's my last day here. I have intensive care experience so I'm being redeployed to the Covid ward.'

'Crikey! Are you looking forward to that?'

'With some trepidation! I'll get some training, apparently, but hopefully it will all come flooding back to me.'

'Oh, well good luck!'

She hands me a booklet about breast reconstruction and a leaflet with the breast care nurses' details.

Neither Steve nor I know quite what to think and say as we make our way back to the car. What can you say? We drive straight home.

11:35
I email my line manager.

From: Wray Marisa
To: Alison
Subject: RE: Breast clinic on Friday

Hi Alison,

The news today was worse than I expected but no immediate action needed.

I have low-grade DCIS but because such a large area of my breast is involved, if they do nothing there is a high chance that it will become invasive. Mastectomy is the recommended treatment (lumpectomy not possible as it's too wide an area).

They are not doing surgery until after Covid crisis but surgeon said in 6-9 months' time I will need a mastectomy. The recovery time is 6-8 weeks, but at least it will be planned.

That takes us to autumn 2020 or even early 2021.

I am reeling somewhat with the news but on the bright side at least the treatment can be postponed without the risk of shortening my life!

I am taking the rest of the day off as I am having trouble concentrating.

BW
Marisa

11:58

From: Alison
To: Wray Marisa
Subject: RE: Breast clinic on Friday

I am sorry Marisa – I am sure you are reeling especially as you are such a healthy living sort of person, if you know what I mean, and this sort of thing I can only imagine really rocks you.

Good news at least that it won't be life shortening.

Thanks once again for being so supportive to me at the moment – it is really appreciated.

Take as much time off as you need to.

Alison

I'm so glad I have a very understanding boss.

13:00
I somehow manage to have an upbeat conversation with both sisters, my sister-in-law and my mum. Jess in New York is in tears on my behalf (strangely, I have never shed a tear over my cancer from start to finish) and I'm overwhelmed with the love everyone is sending me.

14:00
I'm beside myself. I can't keep my mind still. I spend hours surfing the web, researching breast reconstruction techniques and searching for some sort of solace. I dive with gusto into the Cancer Chat forum and I find it helps. There is a very encouraging post written in the early hours of this morning by a forty-nine year old (I'm forty-seven) who was found to have invasive ductal carcinoma after being invited for her first screening mammogram. Like me, she is a healthy eater, sporty and never smoked. Why is this happening to people like us? Her post is so positive that it gives me hope. She's had her surgery and is recovering well.
I type a reply.

Invasive Ductal Carcinoma

Thanks for the encouragement.

I had the news in breast clinic this morning that I have DCIS and although it's not invasive it is widespread in my L breast so I will need a mastectomy. I will have to wait at least 6 months due to Covid.

It's encouraging to hear that you are doing well. I am 47 so not even old enough for a mammogram. I had bleeding which prompted a 2-week wait referral and several biopsies, and 6 weeks later, here I am.

I work for the NHS so am run off my feet at work. Maybe that's a good thing as it will take my mind off things...

Hugs to you xxx

I receive a lovely reply.

Invasive Ductal Carcinoma

Hi Spooky Cat, glad I could offer some encouragement. Sorry to hear about mastectomy as opposed to lumpectomy but if it clears it out and evicts the bad tenant in your boob then all is well with the world.

The NHS is a powerful machine and when you experience such a process, you see it first-hand albeit from a different side-line from working in it.

I always found that researching responsibly and pushing for answers when asking the right questions really helped me to deal with everything and take it on the chin.

Stay safe, wishing you well!

I'm going round in circles thinking about reconstruction. I'm feeling furious with God for visiting this misfortune upon me. I don't want to lose my breast! I like my breasts! I want to be symmetrical! I'm proud of how well I've kept my body. I may be forty-seven but I could be mistaken for twenty-seven in a bikini (well, maybe early thirties...). My VO2 max is in the 'Excellent' category for my age and I'm already mourning the impending loss of my fitness, figure and body image. I'm angry. I'm really angry. It's all very well being positive, but WTF! I turn to the Cancer Chat forum again.

16:52

Mastectomy and reconstruction advice

Hello!

I was hoping I wouldn't need to come on here but here I am, having learned this morning that I need a mastectomy for widespread DCIS in my L breast. Given the COVID-19 crisis, I will have to wait 6 months or more (no worries, it's not likely to transform into something more invasive in that time). However, I was alarmed to find out that I will lose my entire breast. My boobs are only small and the DCIS is occupying far too much of my breast to make breast conserving surgery possible. My right breast is normal so they will leave it alone.

Can anyone advise me on reconstruction options? None of them look ideal. I have heard implants have high failure/complication rates and don't look or feel normal. I am very sporty so I am also worried that if I have flap reconstruction from either my latissimus dorsi or rectus abdominus muscle, I will be left weak and unable to do the sports I love (hiking, running, swimming, climbing, anything adventurous).

Are there any other intrepid adventurers out there who have had reconstructive surgery? How was it? My body image is suffering big time as I am slim and muscular and love being strong and agile. This has come as a big blow to me. I don't even feel like going out for a run. As you can probably gather, I am still reeling from the news.

Thank you,
Marisa (and Spook the cat)

My state of mind is intolerable. I compulsively devour all the information I possibly can about controversies over the treatment of DCIS and investigate the different subtypes. Mine is micropapillary, which seems to be a law unto itself - it can transform unpredictably into invasive cancer even though it is classed as low grade. I also garner all the information I can find about my surgeon. He receives good reviews, which is reassuring.

Saturday 4 April, 2020
I don't know what to do with myself. Steve is very keen for me to get a second opinion. Where do I start?

10.11
I have a bright idea and message a group from the Christian Medical Fellowship (CMF) via WhatsApp.

> Sorry to bother you all but I need some advice, not to mention prayer. I have just found out that I have widespread but low-grade DCIS in L breast. My surgeon says I need a mastectomy. I am alarmed to say the least. There will be a long wait for surgery of course. My husband wants me to get a second opinion. Does anyone have any advice? Thanks and God bless you all. Marisa x

10:12
A reply already!

I can ask my colleague if you want?

I'm flabbergasted! I jump at the offer. The colleague is an oncologist named Martin, who says I can call him tomorrow. Wow! I feel a little bit encouraged.

11:10

I can't sit still. I text a colleague who I know is at work today. Maybe she'll be free for a coffee. I need company.

> Hi Amanda. News yesterday was crappy crappy crappy. Breast surgeon says I need a mastectomy. No urgency as is low-grade DCIS but my goodness it was not what I was hoping for! How is work going today? Marisa x

> **Omg Marisa I'm so sorry to hear that. I'm assuming you are in total shock right now. Loads of love for that, not what you needed to hear I'm sure xxxx. If I can help with anything whenever just let me know. How are you 2? Probably feels very surreal. xx**

> If you can hang on at work for a few mins I'd love a coffee! Have machine in my office. Steve is really struggling and has gone for a walk as I was still in bed!

> **Yes defo. Will head there in 10 mins, then will pop into Crisis team. Should be free by 11.45. I have rooibos tea bags too. x**

Yes! Something to do. Someone to see. I jump on my bike and cycle up the hill to the hospital. I'm so lucky that I live this close.

I pop my head in to say hello to the teams who are working today. There are two members of staff from each team on site at weekends now. They all occupy the big office which usually houses the Memory and Later Life team - the team I work in - so it's very familiar.

'Hi!' I smile at them. 'I'm not working today. Just popped in to have a coffee with Amanda. Anyone want an espresso or a cappuccino?' I have a couple of takers. This is good. I'm absorbed in working the coffee machine.

'Nice to see you all. I'm on next Saturday so may see some of you then,' I say as I hand out the coffees before heading to Amanda's office. I realise that as long as I'm interacting with people, my mind doesn't have to go down the intolerable route of thinking about my predicament.

Amanda is a complete star. She cuts straight to the chase and asks me how on earth I'm coping and takes a psychiatrist's interest in how I'm feeling. It's just what I need right now. I think I can survive until tomorrow.

Chapter 7

Desperately Seeking Succour

Sunday 5 April, 2020
10:00
I call Martin, the oncologist.
  'Hello, is that Martin?'
  'Speaking.'
  'Thank you so much for letting me call you. I've just been diagnosed with DCIS and I'm desperate for some help.'
  'So I've heard, You must be in shock right now.'
  'Yes, I feel awful - my mind's all over the place. My husband's finding it hard to get his head around it, too. The worst thing is that we were just told at the clinic on Friday that they'd review me in three months' time and that was it. I've rather been left reeling.'
  'So you've been diagnosed with low-grade DCIS?'
  'Yes, I know it's quite safe for me to wait a few months for surgery but it's the fact that there is no plan, and no one knows when surgery is going to resume that is doing my head in.'
  'Yes, I quite understand. As doctors we always like to have a plan, don't we? It must be horrible to be at the receiving end of what's happening in the NHS at the moment.'
  'Do you think it would be possible for me to get a second opinion? I'm finding it hard to think straight. At least if I get a second opinion I'll feel as though I'm doing something!'
  'I can't believe that all surgery has just ground to a halt all over the country. I know some NHS breast surgeons who are trying to collaborate and operate in 'cold sites' - private hospitals which are Covid-free. If you like I could ask around and see if any of them would be willing to see you for a second opinion?'
  'That sounds hopeful. Surely all non-Covid services in the NHS can't just grind to a halt? That would be a disaster.'
  'I know.'

'Is it normal to experience terrible anxiety when you get a cancer diagnosis? I'm not afraid of death as such but it's the unknown - not having a plan - that has turned me into a jibbering wreck.'

'Oh, getting a cancer diagnosis is bad enough at the best of times, let alone at the moment. I'm not surprised you're in an anxious state.'

'Thanks for being so understanding. So would you be able to see if one of the surgeons you know could give me a second opinion?'

'Yes, leave it with me and I will text you before the end of the week.'

'Thank you so much! Oh, before you go, would you mind having a talk to my husband?

'Of course, no problem.'

I hand the phone over to Steve. Martin is a godsend. He listens to Steve's concerns and answers all of his questions.

We both feel as though we are getting somewhere. Maybe we will be able to make a plan sooner rather than later. Or should I go private? A friend from medical school became a breast surgeon. I lost touch with her years ago but I wonder if I can guess her email address. She might be able to help.

16:08
My lucky guess is rewarded by a reply.

From: Alison (Ali)
To: Wray Marisa
Subject: Breast cancer advice

Hi Marisa,

You guessed email correctly good to hear from you has been too long but sorry to hear your news. We are too young! And difficult at any time but especially so in these days of Corona. Must be so tough.

From your description it sounds like treatable disease and you will be fine and live to 100 or beyond. If the surgeon has advised a mastectomy, then that will be what is required as it isn't recommended lightly. Half of the breast involved and biopsy of 2 distinct areas - I would agree.

You therefore have 3 options:
1. Simple mastectomy – takes an hour, home same or next day, wear pad in your bra, get back to exercise 4-6 weeks
2. Skin-sparing mastectomy and immediate reconstruction with silicone implant behind the pectoral muscle and usually some mesh at the bottom. 'Subpectoral' takes 2-3 hours. In hospital a couple of days. Can take up to a year for implant to settle in and move a little and shape improve. Should be low-risk complications as you are fit - 5% risk of losing it. Still back to full exercise 6-8 weeks.
3. Skin-sparing mastectomy and immediate reconstruction with silicone implant placed just under the skin with mesh over the top. 'Prepectoral' is a newer technique with advantage that doesn't damage pectoral muscle and if it goes wrong you just have it taken out. Not everywhere may do this though. Similar recovery to 2 but less pain and therefore potentially quicker.

I don't think you would want a latissimus dorsi flap and not enough am sure for an abdominal flap.

I would probably go for 1 or 3!!

Don't worry about the recovery - you will be fine.

Got to be done.

Am sure you will get good advice from your team but you may have a delay in getting your surgery anyway at the moment as operating lists have been cut. Try not to worry about any delays, you have time to get this sorted out and make the decisions.

Tell me your phone number and will give you a call. Need details on the husband too and how you met and everything else you have been up to!

Lots of love,

Ali

It's been at least ten years since I've been in touch with Ali. A lot has happened in both our lives since then, including me meeting and marrying Steve. I'm overcome by how kind and helpful everyone is being. Thank God for friends, colleagues and family!

Monday 6 April, 2020
11:00
I make an enquiry with a private breast clinic. Who knows, they might be doing reconstructions sooner rather than later. Wonder how much it will cost?

I think I will explode if I keep surfing the Web. I know, I'll text Josie.

Hurray, she's free! We meet on the Helm for a socially distanced walk. It's a bit hard to follow French spoken through a face mask but I just about manage. I massively value her lived experience of breast cancer. She knows just what it feels like to be in my shoes.

Tuesday 7 April, 2020
I'm supposed to be doing medical school stuff today but I just can't keep my mind still. I've already informed the director of medical studies and my co-director of third-year medical students about my situation, and they both tell me to take as much time off as I need. Why can't I take time off? I don't feel as if I can allow myself to do so. I feel so responsible for everyone and everything.

My browsing history from today includes:
- Adjustment to Cancer: Anxiety and Distress

- Manual for the State-Trait Anxiety Inventory
- Identification of anxiety and depression symptoms in patients with cancer
- Screening for Distress in Breast Cancer
- The Psychosocial Distress Questionnaire - Breast Cancer
- Development of the Psychosocial Distress Questionnaire
- Psychometric Properties of the Patient Health Questionnaire
- Screening for Emotional Distress in Cancer Patients: A Systematic Review of Assessment Instruments

You can guess where my preoccupation lies today! Working from home is all very well but my self-discipline goes out the window.

Wednesday 8 April, 2020
There's some relief to being back in the hospital. Many of my consultant colleagues are working from home but I come in for my clinical work. It makes me feel more normal. I have a steady stream of team members entering my office through the morning to liaise about patients. My brain appreciates clicking back into clinical decision-making mode. It means I don't have to think about anything else.

Wednesday afternoon is my allocated session for teaching psychiatry to medical students. I was appointed undergraduate (UG) lead for psychiatry at our NHS Trust in 2014. This role is in addition to my clinical work and it keeps me on my toes. It also fits in well with my part-time job as Year Three Co-director at Lancaster Medical School. Third-year students spend seven weeks learning psychiatry and I'm in charge of making sure it all goes swimmingly. I also hope that they learn how to talk to people who are experiencing mental illness, and to recognise the signs and symptoms. Who knows, they may even consider psychiatry as a future career specialty. It's the best one, after all (not that I'm biased)!

13:34
I email Nick, Jo and Donna, my fantastic medical education team colleagues.

From: Marisa Wray
To: Nick, Jo, Donna
Subject: RE: rotation 4

Hi Nick et al,

The materials you've prepared look brilliant, thank you so much.

Clinical work is busy here, so I have not been able to spend any time on UG stuff recently. However, there is a website with pooled resources from all the UG psych leads: https://medschoolpsychiatry.com/

I am a bit all over the place at the moment as I found out on Friday that I have breast cancer and need a mastectomy. It won't be any time soon due to Covid but it is doing my head in rather.

If I don't respond to emails quickly it's either because I'm snowed under with clinical work or my head is in a spin!

Shall we have a virtual get together soon?

BW
Marisa

13:47
I receive a reply from Nick.

From: Nick
To: Wray Marisa
Subject: RE: rotation 4

Oh God – sorry to hear that. I'm assuming the mastectomy can be postponed within reason? I think with Covid the uncertainty is sometimes more unhelpful… if I knew we'd be

in lockdown until August 20 then for next 6 months -
minimal travel, no overseas travel, everyone wears masks and
no more than 20 people in a supermarket at any one time – it
would be grim but at least we'd know what to prepare for!!!

Yeah, will try and sort out a skype link or similar

Don't worry about the UG stuff - Jo and I and the rest of the
team can manage.

BW
Nick

13:55
And Jo.

From: Jo
To: Wray Marisa
Subject: RE: rotation 4

Hi Marisa

I can't believe your news - you must be in total shock. What
an awful situation to be in waiting for treatment. I really
don't know what to say, I'm so sorry you're having to deal
with this.

Don't worry in the least about the UG programme - we will
sort it.

Take care, I will be thinking about you xx

13:56
And Donna.

From: Donna
To: Wray Marisa
Subject: RE: rotation 4

Hi Marisa

I am very sorry to hear your news!!! The last time I saw you it all sounded so positive, didn't it? I'm not quite sure how you are managing to work at all, let alone at a time like this.

Donna x

I love my colleagues!

Thursday 9 April, 2020
17:06
I receive a text from Martin the oncologist.

> **Hi Marisa, I've spoken to my surgical colleagues, can you ask GP to refer to Mr T at Hospital B. We will then be able to review the radiology and pathology and make sure we are happy with the timings of operations and whether it should be sooner or later. There is some breast surgery continuing and it is being undertaken at cold sites, ie. done by NHS in private hospitals.**
> **Call me if you need anything, if not we'll talk after MDT. I hope you have a happy Easter.**

19:00
I'm expecting a call. Breast Cancer Now has this excellent service, 'Someone Like Me', where they match you with somebody who has already been through breast cancer. The lady who is due to phone me is my age, was diagnosed with DCIS and underwent a mastectomy with immediate implant reconstruction. She is very sporty, just like I am.

19:30
No phone call. The story of my life...

Friday 10 April, 2020
19:00
The phone rings.

'Hello is that Marisa? I'm so sorry, I was supposed to call you last night but my internet went down and I couldn't access my emails and I had no other way of getting your number. I'm so sorry, are you free to talk now?

'Oh, are you from Someone Like Me?'

We have a reassuring conversation where she emphasises how smoothly her surgery went and how she managed to get back to normal fitness again. OK, deep breath. Maybe it won't be so bad to adjust to a changed body. If others can do it then so can I.

Saturday 11 April, 2020
10:16
I text Martin, the oncologist.

> Thank you, Martin. I made the request to my GP yesterday so hopefully she will get the referral done next week. The waiting and uncertainty are doing my head in! I am at work today which is probably a good thing as it takes my mind off it!
> Have a happy Easter.

In a way it's a relief to be at work. My skills are not being put to their best use, but I spend many hours phoning around pharmacies to see which one happens to be open on Easter Saturday. Why is there a local shortage of every drug I have prescribed today?

'Hello, is that Asda Pharmacy? You have five tablets left? Yes! I will take them!'

That just about sums up my day.

14:30

I've run out of work to do. I'm sitting at my desk. My mind is starting to go berserk again. I start googling cancer helplines. They're all closed over the Easter long weekend. Great! I stumble across the website of Anxiety UK. They've put on extra services this weekend because of Covid. Hurray, they have a live chat which I can access straight away! I immediately sign up and find myself in a text conversation with a counsellor.

He is absolutely brilliant. I feel so validated by our conversation. The power of his words of understanding and encouragement enable me to carry on. One day at a time.

Sunday 12 April, 2020
13:45
I am messaging Amanda on WhatsApp.

How are u doing? Hope u are enjoying some time off work. x

Moments when I feel ok and others when I don't. Work yesterday v busy writing FP10s and chasing up chemists which could fill them! Now got 4 days off - yay! Hope you're having a good weekend xx

Good to know that the weekend shifts aren't in vain... tho sorry you were busy. 4 days off sounds good tho. I can't imagine how it must feel to have to get your head round something so big. I hope you are being really kind to yourself. Sending hugs xxx

This will make you laugh. All the breast cancer helplines are closed over the weekend so yesterday after work I found myself having an online chat with a volunteer at Anxiety UK. They are open all weekend because of Covid! It was actually helpful just to sound off to a complete stranger! xx

That is so rubbish. But very resourceful of u! Sorry u are having such a rough time tho mate. Can talk any time you know xxx

Monday 13 April, 2020
10:45
I call Merryn in Australia. She had triple-negative breast cancer when she was thirty-seven, and ended up having a mastectomy and TRAM-flap reconstruction on both breasts. She now runs a support group for women who have had breast cancer, and is a spiritual therapist who specialises in guided visualisation meditations for healing.

We chat for over an hour. Beauty just emanates from her soul. When she offers to do some guided meditations with me via video on Facebook Messenger, I leap at the chance. How about tomorrow? Yes! Grab, grab, grab. I'm taking any help that's offered to me.

12:15
It's only ten degrees but the sun is shining. What can I do to send a 'fuck you' message to the nastiness in my breast? Hmmm, I wonder...

12:35
The sun sparkles on the water of the river Kent. I'm sweating, I walked fast to get here. Do I dare? There's no one around. The riverbank is deserted. I'm in a sunny glade, a break in the trees where limestone slabs slope gently down into the water. It's very inviting. Right, nothing else for it. Off with my clothes and in I get. Ah! Gasp! Swim! Cold water bites at every inch of my flesh. Oh, it's wonderful!

I swim one hundred metres or so upstream. I haven't forgotten how to do breaststroke, though it's been a while. Take that, bad boob! Before I get out, I take a selfie of the inane grin plastered across my face - nothing can wipe it off. My skin is tingling. I'm zinging. Oh yeah!

I text my photo to Steve.

Crazy but happy! I love you. xxxxxxxx

You are crazy. Love you. xxxxx

Tuesday 14 April, 2020
12:00
I'm lying on a mat in the garden in the sunshine. It's sufficiently warm for me not to need a coat. Merryn's talking to me from my phone screen, and I have my earphones in.

I close my eyes. I breathe deeply - in through the nose for six then out through the mouth. Once I am deeply relaxed, she prompts me to go within my body and ask it where it wants me to look.

I can feel the tip of my right shoulder. I look inside it and see a black and red mesh. A muscle is twitching. Around it is blue and yellow fluid. This is where my tension is coming from. Why do my muscles have a mind of their own? I see a paintbrush paint a swathe of yellow against a bright blue sky. I'm transported to Egypt. I am climbing an ancient pyramid and I'm out of breath. I feel the sweat prickling on my skin. As I get higher, I see an oasis of green in the distance. I see sand, dry desert and the ruins of an ancient city. I know that I'm connected to all of this through time - the civilisations that have gone before me. I'm three quarters of the way up the pyramid and I love the sense of solitude. No one else is silly enough to come up here. A white dove lands near me. It's as curious about me as I am about it. It's playful. It wants to join me in my high place. I am climbing this pyramid simply because I love going to the top. I have no expectations - I just love to explore.

Back at the bottom of the pyramid, I try to leave but I'm stuck in a doorway feeling full of confusion and fear. I am aware that I'm in awe of the world and I want to climb mountains - I even fly in my dreams. I fear all that will be taken away from me. Now I am tied down. I am decrepit. I see that I am fragmented, frozen and splintered. My body is letting me down.

Merryn gently guides me back down my timeline to my twenty-year-old self. I tell the younger me not to worry so much.

To be who she is rather than try to be who she isn't. Next, I visit my thirty-year-old self and smile at her because she sees such hope for a bright future. Then I feel deep sorrow for my forty-year-old self who has just realised that she is biologically dead. She can't have children.

Merryn takes me back to the top of the pyramid where my dove has transformed into a wise old woman. I ask her why I'm here.

'You're here to live,' she tells me.

'What is my purpose?' I ask.

'To inspire,' she replies.

'Why couldn't I have children?'

'You need to be able to empathise with people whose worst nightmare has come true,' she answers. The old woman spreads her wings and flies away.

Next, Merryn guides me to my future self. I'm feeling whole and content again. I am contemplative and I listen. I'm also doing what I love: hiking, always exploring, always being curious. My future self advises me to keep my sense of humour and to accept help from my family and friends.

I return to the door that was blocking my way out of the pyramid and find that it is gone. The sun is now shining in, and I *fly* out. I am soaring over mountains, valleys and rivers…

What on earth was THAT! Merryn says my guidance is to accept myself as I am and follow my heart. She says I must be confident in who I am and what I do for once I believe in myself I will spread my wings and soar!

I feel elated for a while, then settle into a feeling of wellbeing. It lasts a couple of days before I'm back in my anxious state.

Wednesday 15 April, 2020
09:00
I receive a reply from the private breast clinic.

Dear Dr Wray,

We have received your enquiry. Would like to know what you have been advised? Lumpectomy or mastectomy (breast removal)? They are generally advising against reconstruction as this makes the surgery more complex, given Covid situation. It would also make it a lot more expensive.

Initial consultation fee is £220 and the guideline cost for the surgery including hospital fee, surgeon's fee and anaesthetist fee is £8000 (includes post-op follow up).

If you still want to go ahead, we can fit you in soon.

Kind regards.

You've gotta be joking! Eight grand and that's without the reconstruction! Scrap that idea!

Friday 17 April, 2020
12:23
I text Martin the oncologist.

Hi Martin, hope this finds you well. Do you know when the MDT is likely to be? I'm struggling with all the waiting! Thanks.

I've spoken to Mr T and he's agreed to look at your findings. The MDT list for Tuesday hasn't been circulated yet and the coordinator isn't answering. I'll check later on today. Hopefully next Tuesday. Will update you by end of day.

19:27
I receive a text from Martin.

I've been checking emails and chasing the coordinator who wasn't answering emails or phone this afternoon. I'll have to check on Monday for the finalised list. I'm sorry I couldn't confirm tonight. However, there are priority surgical lists happening in the local private hospitals. I'll check again on Monday onwards. If there is a need to operate, I'm sure we can find a slot soon. Sorry not to be more specific today.

Monday 20 April, 2020
12:00
I have my second guided meditation with Merryn.

I'm living in a castle. I'm in my favourite room - it's at the top of the tower, filled with sunlight and has a 360-degree panorama. I become aware that I need to visit the dungeons. The stairs leading down to them are uneven and slippery. I feel sad and apprehensive... guilty that I can't bring myself to come here more often. The prisoners might want something from me that I can't give them.

I open the door. The cells are separated by bars and the men inside them are scruffy. I can't see their faces. The man in cell one couldn't pay his taxes. He doesn't blame me for being held there but I still feel guilty that I have neither visited him nor petitioned for his release. I ask him how he is feeling. He says he's feeling hopeful that his sentence will come to an end soon.

'Yes,' I say, 'it's just a few more months now.'

The man in cell two is serving a life sentence for murder. He feels resigned. He says that it's possible to serve a life sentence and keep your sanity. He recites Shakespeare to himself because it's beautiful and he can live other people's lives through his imagination. I'm awed by him because he's not wallowing. He was going to receive a death sentence but they decided to give him a worse punishment - to languish. But in fact, it's not worse because he has found something that has given him joy and meaning.

In the third cell is a hermit. He chooses to be there because he likes it there. It is quiet and he is blind. He doesn't need to see so it doesn't matter to him that it's dark. He is a mystic. Even though

95

he can't see, he has inner sight. He can see what's happening in people's lives and sends help in various forms, usually as birds.

He looks inside me and sees love in my heart, but he says my heart and its beat are out of sync. He shows me scenes from my past. The first one is me as a nervous, shy little girl, who feels out of sync with the world. She must pluck up the courage to join gym club because she fears rejection. However, it turns out the teacher is delighted to have her. She is good at gym club. I can see now that nobody was judging her.

Next, I see the same little girl in the school playground, feeling torn because her friends are being mean to a new girl. My child self feels cowardly and guilty, wanting to both please her friends and welcome the new girl. I now see that she was not cowardly but a diplomat in the making.

Now she is older and has been accepted to do her PhD. She feels hopeful and excited. She has no long-term plan but is relieved to be doing something that makes her heart sing. She is taking a break to do research because her body and mind couldn't tolerate doctoring. I can see that it's OK not to know what's coming next.

My heartbeat is regular again.

The meaning of cells one and two are obvious. My sentence (waiting for surgery) will come to an end in a few months and being sentenced to a lifetime of punishment is my perception of a life without children. But the prisoner can still find plenty of beauty in the world and meaning in life. Even the interminable waiting for surgery has brought me back to doing what I love: art, running and wild swimming. It has also led me to meditation.

Merryn sees two lessons from the hermit in cell three. The first is seeing the beauty in myself and understanding my true value. The second is the importance of following my truth, instead of trying to fit a mould. Working as a doctor, I became physically and mentally ill. I took a chance by dropping out, not knowing what was coming next; yet from that came the opportunity to immerse myself in beautiful science and gain a PhD.

Tuesday 21 April, 2020
18:00
I text Martin the oncologist.

Hi Martin. Any idea whether they managed to discuss me at MDT today? Thanks.

There's been a problem with the referral, I had access to the list this morning (it's normally only finalised on the day). There's not been any evidence of the referral. We've checked directly with the consultant's secretary and the two-week rule centre in case it was misdirected. We realise about the delay and we'll try and get our team to liaise at next week's MDT. Will you ask your GP to confirm where they sent the referral and cc me in. I am sorry for the delay but I'll try to expedite things for you. I'm sorry, you will feel quite let down and quite frustrated. Increasingly surgical lists are happening and so the likelihood of an operation in a cold site is strong. I'll let you know tomorrow if there is any update from my end. Very sorry.

Thanks. Would you happen to know whether any implant reconstructions are going ahead at the same time as mastectomy? I'd much rather have it done at the same time than have a mastectomy, be completely flat on one side, lose my skin and have far fewer options for reconstruction in the long run. I've been reading up on micropapillary DCIS and even the low-grade ones seem to behave unpredictably and can have micro-infiltrations. I'm still getting discharge and it itches. Thank you!

The surgeons I've spoken to are oncoplastic surgeons and good ones at that. They would be best fixed to advise. I'll get them to talk directly. I'll also tell them about the discharge. Regardless of where we're up to, I'll contact you tomorrow.

Wednesday 22 April, 2020
11:30

Hi Marisa, I have spoken with Mr P and some of the other surgeons. It goes without saying that none of us are comfortable with the delays. He's going to speak to you especially in the light of your persistent pruritus and discharge. We have also discussed sharing capacity. All the surgeons will work within the association of breast surgeons' current guidelines for which ops should be done at the moment. This impacts on reconstructions in particular.
Let me know if he doesn't call in next day or so.

Thanks Martin. I just got a call from breast clinic to say Mr P will call me tomorrow.

Let me know how it goes.

Thursday 23 April, 2020
09:30

Hi Martin,, good conversation with Mr P. He reassured me that I'd be terribly unlucky if cancer became invasive in next few months and that when they restart reconstructions, I will be first on the list! Just a waiting game for how long the pandemic will cause reconstruction surgery to be banned. I would far rather have the reconstruction done straight away so will wait and keep fingers crossed.

If things change in terms of symptoms get back in touch with him. I'll still chase MDT review as well, just for completeness.

Monday 27 April, 2020
08:48

Hi Marisa. Your scans etc will be discussed at MDT on Tuesday, if you're happy for us to do so, giving a second opinion. I'll let you know what the team thinks. I'll discuss the options with you, and then you can decide if it changes things enough to see someone else. Is that ok?

Yes, thanks Martin that's perfect. I've been doing some homework and reading up on micropapillary DCIS. There is not much literature on it but am I right in thinking it behaves a bit differently from other types of DCIS? More likely to have micro-infiltrations even if low-grade. Discharge has slowed down again. I keep checking the ABS website and there is no word yet on whether reconstructions are likely to resume any time soon. Psychologically the impact on me of having to have a mastectomy with delayed reconstruction would be horrible. Basically, it's a question of weighing up the risk of indefinite delay to get mastectomy and implant reconstruction done in one go against the psychological impact (and poorer aesthetic result plus longer off work in long run) of mastectomy and delayed reconstruction. Thank you for hearing me out!

Let's see what they say, if both groups of surgeons have the same advice this will give some reassurance going forward. Be in touch soon.

Monday 27 April, 2020
12:00
I have my third guided meditation with Merryn.
I'm floating down a river on my back, enjoying the changing scenery. I pass through different places: the Grand Canyon - an eagle circles overhead; then China - I see pagodas, hanging trees and people doing Tai Chi on the riverbank.

I begin to hear tinkling music in the water and I realise this is enchanted water with healing properties. The daughters of the air from Hans Christian Anderson's *The Little Mermaid* are there. They appear as clear beings of light and they have come to reassure me.

The river enters a calm sea and I am floating among the natural rock arches off the coast of Calabria in Italy. I see a rock arch looming. It is there just for me. As I pass beneath it, I receive a full-body scan. There's something in my left breast. The architecture inside it has been disturbed. It's been working too hard. Too many arches have tried to build themselves, have become stuck and are breaking down. The arches represent industriousness and striving. I know I can heal by lovingly dismantling them, starting from the top and working my way down.

At the top is my expectation of myself – I have high standards for myself. Growing up, my mantra was 'Good, better, best. Never let it rest. Until your good is better and your better is best.' If I didn't stick to it, I felt I wasn't achieving, and I was letting people down. I realise that I have done my best and I no longer have to live by that mantra. My best doesn't need to be perfect. Nor does my breast.

Tuesday 28 April 2020
09:50
I text Martin the oncologist.

> Hi Martin. A friend attended a planning meeting at Morecambe Bay Hospitals yesterday about restoration of elective surgery. They said it will not happen until end of July/beginning of August. Not sure if other Trusts are also saying the same? The glimmer of hope I had after NHS England's announcement yesterday has vanished!

Let's see after MDT. The goal posts move all the time.

Martin has the patience of a saint! After the MDT he calls me to say that Mr T will call me tomorrow or Thursday. Result!

Someone has sent me a Facebook post for a bit of light relief:

The Rules
For the sake of clarification, here are those lockdown rules one more time:

1. You MUST NOT leave the house for any reason, but if you have a reason, you can leave the house.

2. Masks are useless at protecting you against the virus, but you may have to wear one because it can save lives, but they may not work, but they may be mandatory, but maybe not.

3. Shops are closed, except those shops that are open.

4. You must not go to work, but you can get another job and go to work.

5. You should not go to the doctor's or to the hospital unless you have to go there, unless you are too poorly to go there.

6. This virus can kill people, but don't be scared of it. It can only kill those people who are vulnerable or those people who are not vulnerable. It's possible to contain and control it, sometimes, except that sometimes it leads to a global disaster.

7. Gloves won't help, but they can still help so wear them sometimes, or not.

8. STAY HOME, but it's important to go out.

9. There is no shortage of groceries in the supermarkets, but there are many things missing. Sometimes you won't need loo rolls, but you should buy some just in case you need them.

10. Animals are not affected, but there was a cat that tested positive in Belgium in February when no one had been tested, plus a few tigers here and there.

11. Stay two metres away from tigers (see point 10).

12. You will have many symptoms if you get the virus, but you can also get symptoms without getting the virus, get the virus without having any symptoms or be contagious

without having symptoms, or be non-contagious with symptoms... it's a sort of lucky/unlucky dip.

13. To help protect yourself you should eat well and exercise, but eat whatever you have on hand as it's better not to go to the shops, unless you need toilet roll or a fence panel.

14. It's important to get fresh air but don't go to parks but go for a walk. But don't sit down, except if you are old, but not for too long or if you're not old but need to sit down. If you do sit down don't eat your picnic, unless you've had a long walk, which you are/aren't allowed to do if you're old.

15. Don't visit old people but take care of the old people and bring them food and medication.

16. If you are sick, you can go out when you are better but anyone else in your household can't go out when you are better, unless they need to go out.

17. You can get restaurant food delivered to the house. These deliveries are safe. But groceries you bring back to your house have to be decontaminated outside for three hours including frozen pizza.

18. You can't see your older mother or grandmother, but they can take a taxi and meet an older taxi driver.

19. You are safe if you maintain the safe social distance when out, but you can't go out with friends or strangers at the safe social distance.

20. The virus remains active on different surfaces for two hours... or four hours... or six hours... I mean days, not hours. But it needs a damp environment. Or a cold environment that is warm and dry... in the air, as long as the air is not plastic.

21. The number of coronavirus-related deaths will be announced daily but we don't know how many people are infected as they are only testing those who are almost dead to find out if that's what they will die of. The people who die of coronavirus who aren't counted, won't or will be counted but maybe not.

22. We should stay in lockdown until the virus stops infecting people, but it will only stop infecting people if we all get infected so it's important that we get infected and some don't get infected.

23. You can join your neighbours for a street party and turn your music up for an outside disco and your neighbours won't call the police. People in another street are allowed to call the police about your music whilst also having a party which you are allowed to call the police about.

24. No business will go down due to coronavirus except those businesses that will go down due to Coronavirus.

15:00

I have my first of twenty free counselling sessions via Zoom with a therapist from Cancer Care. She doesn't beat around the bush. We get straight to business. I think I'm going to like her.

Chapter 8

Second Opinion

Wednesday 30 April, 2020
I'm working from home today and Steve and I take a break for a walk on the Helm.

My mobile rings.

'Hello?'

'Hello is that Dr Wray?'

'Yes, it's Marisa.'

'This is Mr T, breast surgeon from Hospital B. Is now a good time to talk?

'Yes!'

'I think you've already spoken to Martin? I know there was a bit of a delay with us getting the referral but we did discuss your case at our MDT yesterday. I think you were keen to get a second opinion. The thing that strikes me is the pathology report was rather inconclusive, and we agreed as a team that we would like to see the actual slides before we make a management plan. It seems to me that we're not really sure what we are dealing with.'

'Yes, the pathology report said one area "could be" low-grade DCIS and the other area was "more likely to represent" low-grade DCIS,' I explain. 'It doesn't exactly inspire confidence! It's on the basis of that, that they're recommending a mastectomy.'

'It's possible there is an invasive cancer there which hasn't been sampled. I would recommend a further biopsy of the most densely calcified area. The thing is that you need to decide whether you want to transfer your care to us. Are you in Kendal? Burnley's about an hour and a quarter's drive from you.'

'Yes, I'll do it. I'd like to transfer my care please.'

'Great, then we will arrange for the pathology slides to be transferred across so we can actually have a look at them ourselves.'

· 'Thank you. Do you think it's possible that I don't even need a mastectomy? If the changes only 'might be' DCIS?'

'No, no, that's not what I'm saying. I think it highly likely that we will find DCIS there but we need more clarity on what we are dealing with in order to make the best management plan possible. The more information we have, the better.'

'OK, thanks. How soon will the biopsy be?'

'Within the next week or two. You'll either get a phone call or a text message.'

'OK then, thank you. Bye.'

Oh yes! Things are moving. I have a new spring in my step as we head for home. As we descend on the road, a car passes. It's some friends from the mountaineering club whom we've not seen in a while. I'm not sure they were prepared for my answer to the perennial 'How are you?' question.

Thursday 7 May, 2020

One week later, Steve and I are discovering the delights of Hospital B. The breast unit is old and tired, and almost deserted. I'm not in the mood for conversation so I sit at the opposite end of the enormous, featureless waiting room from its other occupants. Most of the seats are marked with a big cross in case anyone is tempted to sit too close. I sit and stare into space.

'Is my husband allowed to accompany me?' I had asked when I booked the appointment. 'I'm not supposed to drive after the biopsy so he'll have to drive me there but will he have to wait in the car?'

'Yes, I'm afraid no one other than the patient is allowed into the clinic.'

'But what if it's hot? He'll expire if he has to sit in the car!'

'Then he can get out and go for a walk round the area.'

Over the next few weeks Steve and I would become very familiar with the petrol station just along the road from the hospital which, we are sure, does great business serving Costa coffee to hospital staff and breast-unit patients. Just around the corner is a grocery store boasting a beautiful display of begonias, which Steve reckons will be just the thing for our garden. That's if they survive the heat in the back of the car.

A nurse comes to fetch me, and I tell her that I'm a bit of an old hand at this VAB business. They're just about to stab me with the local anaesthetic when I hear a 'phut' sound. Oh dear, the VAB machine seems to have broken! I am extricated from the stereotaxy machine and ushered into a comfortable side room.

'Sorry about this. We hope it's just the fuse.'

I am serene. I swapped my Thursday clinic to Wednesday this week so I have the whole day off. I set to work filling out a questionnaire on my phone about coping during Covid. It's a research study in which I'm taking part.

'Would you like a cup of tea?' the nurse asks me.

'Yes please!'

'You're not in a hurry, are you? If you can wait, we are hoping that it is just the fuse and the maintenance man is going to come within the next couple of hours.'

'That's fine. What if it's not the fuse?'

'Then I'm afraid you'll have to come back another day. Sorry.'

An hour and a half later I'm back on the machine. It was the fuse after all. Hurray!

All done. Now the familiar wait for more results.

Friday 8 May, 2020

Today is VE Day bank holiday and the sun is shining. I get my ukulele out and we have a socially distanced street party outside our front drive. Prosecco is a good lubricator of conversation and I receive plenty of sympathy over my predicament with my misbehaving boob. I love to sing and play, and I even draw some applause from neighbours a few garden fences away.

Monday 11 May, 2020
12:00

Meditation with Merryn begins with us revisiting my left breast.

I'm back in the sea, floating under the natural arches. This time they are made of honeycomb and I can see the individual hexagons fitting together. Bees are there making honey; they are successful, industrious, happy. The tops of the arches are now strong and well-built, but the sides are mucky. They need Royal Jelly so I ask the bees to apply some. There has been doubt and a lack of pride in building and the arches have been neglected.

I can see that at one time my own doubt had led to physical illness, forcing me to give up my job as a doctor in order to slow down. I had to just be. And do tasks that required no intellectual effort at all, like painting and gardening. They felt empty but restoring, made me feel calm and gave me a sense of pride. I had been a square peg in a round hole and I did what I had to do even though it meant defying people's expectations of me. I needed time to recuperate, think about my next step, contemplate what brings me joy and excitement, see where my talents lie and how to use my strength. I see that my strength is my insatiable, intellectual curiosity.

Now I am looking at the path ahead of me. It's lined with blackberry bushes, which have thorns. It's going to be challenging but I am armed with secateurs and gloves, and I am good at seeing ways to get through. I can make sense of the blackberry bushes and need to get rid of the thorns in order access the roots. I realise the whole structure of the briar is beautiful, including its thorns - the stalk is just doing its job of putting out new shoots, and it is plentiful. I need to trim it to clear my path. Make it smoother and easier. I feel frustrated because it's going to take such a long time.

My PhD supervisor appears. He tells me that I have sufficient time and the result will be worth the effort. He says there is no shortcut, that I have to do it properly. Just like my 'time out' from being a doctor. This is what liberated me from my dilemma, led me to my PhD and finding the work I love.

I return to the natural arch. The neglect and lack of pride have vanished from its walls. It is looking rather glorious. I realise the structure underneath is as strong as ever. I have learned there is a time for everything and no experience – good or bad – is wasted. Self-doubt is natural and it needn't be paralysing. I am stronger than I thought.

Tuesday 12 May, 2020
17:25
I receive a call from breast clinic. That's kind of them to call straight after the MDT. I wasn't expecting the results to come through so fast. I'm impressed!
They inform me that the biopsy showed low-grade DCIS.

I text Mum.

> Just got a call to say they got biopsy results and surgeon will call me to discuss tomorrow. They only found more low-grade DCIS but recommend mastectomy and immediate reconstruction as before. Might have MRI to further help plan surgery. So good news. No one knows when reconstruction will be possible as is a global thing due to Covid. xxx

Wednesday 13 May, 2020
18:17
I receive a text from Mum.

Did surgeon call???

> Yes. They want to do MRI scan in next couple of weeks. He says I can safely wait for surgery and to have reconstruction done at same time. No word yet on when it can happen. Not likely before autumn. xxx

Monday 18 May, 2020
12:00
In today's meditation with Merryn, I'm swimming in the river. I spy something on the riverbed. I dive to pick it up and see that it's an emerald. It's not easy being green. The emerald shows me that I am here to embrace the world and all living things. Just as green is a life-giving colour, I give through my work. I love to understand things. I love to listen to people. I am always curious.

My heart seeks to understand the human experience - what it is to be human.

I see that connections are like a spider's web: sometimes you need to feel your way along because you can't always see. Sometimes, my family cannot see that my happiness - or lack thereof - is not a reflection on them. They mustn't feel responsible for it, nor can I allow them to put pressure on me to be happy. I have to be me. I can tolerate pain - pain is there to teach us something.

Wednesday 20 May, 2020
As the days go by at work, I'm finding it harder and harder to concentrate. My self-confidence is waning and I'm worried my colleagues are fed up with me. My counsellor suggests asking the people I know well to write down five words that best describe me. I feel like a bit of a nincompoop but it might help to improve my mood so OK, here goes!

These are the words that the eleven members of my team here this morning each come up with: kind (six), intelligent (six), caring (three), compassionate (two), empathic (two), approachable (two), supportive (two), beautiful (two), talented (two), knowledgeable (two), lovely (two), unique, passionate, hard-working, strong, calming, cheerful, accommodating, entertaining, educational, gentle, easy to talk to, fun, musical, thorough, measured, mindful, insightful, adventurous, good teacher, artistic, energetic, radiant, fabulous!

I perform the same exercise with my family, whose words are remarkably similar. Spooky. You might ask whether it would not be more useful to ask for three positive words and two 'for improvement' but I tend to discount the positive and dwell on the negative. I feel hopeful that people aren't so fed up with me after all.

15:26
I receive a WhatsApp message from Di, my sister-in-law.

Hi Mis, how's it going? Did you get other biopsy results? Xxx

Biopsy showed more DCIS. Going for MRI scan tomorrow to gauge extent of the actual cancer as opposed to the precancerous changes which are also there. Still no news on resumption of surgery. Feeling a bit rubbish with it all and worrying how long work is going to be able to put up with me not firing on all 4 cylinders.
How are you? Gathered you were having a crisis on Sunday evening? Sending lots of love. xxx

Sorry to hear that Mis, really think you should be able to take time off to deal with all this. It's a lot to process without the traumatic covid situ we find ourselves in magnifying it all.
All ok this end, we have good days and bad [with home schooling]. Don't think the heat helps! Sending lots of hugs and love xxxx

Thursday 21 May, 2020
08:45
It takes me a little time to find the MRI department. The big MRI sign on the outside of the building does not seem to correspond with the entrance to the department, which is around the corner. Never mind, I'm early. The whole place is deserted. Eerie.

I'm quite familiar with MRI scanners - I used one for research once - but I'm not prepared for the contraption I'm introduced to for my breast MRI. The radiographer explains that I will be in the scanner for the best part of twenty-five minutes, and they will inject contrast into my vein about halfway through. No drama, I have good veins in the back of my hand. She also says it's imperative that I lie completely still in the scanner.

Why is it that when you're told to lie still you feel the overwhelming urge to wriggle? I'm lying on my front, my chest supported by a contraption which allows my boobs to hang in space. It's obviously made for all sizes, as there's plenty of space in between my boobs and the surrounding support.

Thankfully the experience isn't too bad. As I leave, I can see the images on the screen outside. Can I have a look? No, they need to be processed and it will be a week or two before the results are ready. A familiar refrain.

17:48
I receive a message on WhatsApp from Di, my sister-in-law.

How did it go today, Mis? Hope you didn't have any fuse dramas etc. xxx

All went without a glitch thanks! xxx

Hope you don't have to wait too long for results. xxx

Yes, though there is precious little they can do once we have the results.

So frustrating for you Mis.

Monday 25 May, 2020
Struggling today. Steve and I both feel down and exhausted. Thankfully it's meditation day.

12:00
Our meditation session today is different. Merryn senses that I need to rest so instead of her usual method of guiding me within for the answers to her questions, I lay back in silence and receive a deep healing.

I'm surrounded by royal blue light. It guides me to my heart. I didn't realise it was looking so withered and shrivelled. The light soothes me. Mary, the mother of Jesus, is here. She sends the blue light through the crown of my head. I feel so nurtured and loved. God's love feels unconditional, deep and powerful. I witness a star being born. Its colours are bright. I can see the Earth from space. I give it a big hug. I feel still and peaceful.

Tuesday 26 May, 2020
I'm feeling hopeful that I might get a call from breast clinic this evening. Fingers crossed the MRI results came through and they discussed me in their MDT.

15:30
Mum sends me a WhatsApp message.

Any news re MRI?

Not yet. Xx

18:35
I message her an update.

No word from breast clinic so assume results are not through yet. xxx

Bank Holiday probably delayed results.

Wednesday 27 May, 2020
Our team's 'away day' was cancelled due to Covid so we are having a scaled-down version in smaller groups to socially distance. This afternoon it's the turn of the Early Memory Team, which I have joined for the day. I do a lot of dementia diagnoses with them, so it makes sense.
    My phone rings so I sneak out of the meeting room.
    'Hello, is that Marisa?
    'Yes, hello.'
    'It's Mr T. How are you? Better than I am, I expect…'
    Why does he think that? Things must be bad in his world! 'I'm alright thanks.'

'So we've got your MRI results and the scan shows two possible invasive foci. That means we can't afford to wait too much longer. I'd like to schedule your surgery for the end of June.'

'Wow, will I be able to have the reconstruction at the same time?'

'Yes, as long as we can source the right implant - we don't keep them on the shelf.'

'Brilliant! So what happens now?'

You'll be called for a pre-op a couple of weeks before the op and you'll also have to start self-isolating fourteen days prior.

'OK, so pre-op is likely to be in a couple of weeks' time?

'Should be.'

'Thank you so much! Bye then.'

Yes! Just take the darn thing out! My mood immediately brightens. I've got something to plan for! I feel so much lighter.

I sit through the rest of the afternoon with a smile on my face, my thoughts racing. I love being in planning mode.

16:47
I email my line manager.

From: Wray Marisa
To: Alison
Subject: Update

Hi Alison,

I now have a bit of clarity on my surgery. There are still some unknowns (making sure the implants are in stock and that they can book theatre time in a cold site), but they are aiming to schedule it for the end of June/beginning of July at the latest. My MRI scan showed that there may be some areas of invasive disease so they do not think I can afford to wait any longer.

The current rules for anyone undergoing surgery are for the whole household to self-isolate for 14 days prior to surgery (whether or not anyone has symptoms), which means that I will not be able to leave my home for those 2 weeks. I have been coming in to work physically since the lockdown (other than the week I had symptoms) so it will be quite a change for me. The team knows about this. To be honest, I would like to take those two weeks as sick leave to prepare myself mentally (and physically) for surgery and not to be stressed having to make difficult clinical decisions from home. I have found being physically on site to be hugely important for my wellbeing whilst I am working with the team and making clinical decisions.

The post-op recovery time is 6-8 weeks depending on how it all goes and no complications. So in total I will be absent for at least 2 months.

I need to go for a pre-op sometime in the next couple of weeks, so will have to take a day off for that.

Who do I need to inform of my plans? Of course, once the dates are confirmed I will let you know. I can't say for certain as they may still not be able to go ahead, but I think it likely that I will be off sick from Wednesday 17 June. I have a teaching session planned that day with the GP registrars (I teach them about dementia every year) via Zoom so will still do that but I think I need to be prepared to start self-isolating that day, or even from the Monday of that week.

BW
Marisa

Ah, the sense of relief! I can actually give work some dates and not have to keep saying 'I've been diagnosed with breast cancer. I'm going to be off sick for a mastectomy but I don't know when. I'm sorry, it's doing my head in.' It also legitimises my impending absence. I'm not sure how much longer I can keep going at work.

I'm at breaking point. All being well, my last day of physically being at work will be Friday 12 June. 'Possible invasive foci'. Should I rejoice or should I worry? Ironically, I'm glad there is finally something in my breast that galvanises the surgeon into action. No more indefinite waiting because I can 'afford to'. Now we can't afford to wait any more.

Chapter 9

So Near Yet So Far

Monday 1 June, 2020
I'm trying to stay buoyant. My sense of vitality has returned and I'm feeling hopeful.

12:00
In my meditation with Merryn, I go to a place where I haven't dared to venture before.

I meet with my Auntie Sue, who died from multiple sclerosis a few years ago. She was childless, like me. I see many parallels between our lives. She tells me she came to terms with not having children by throwing herself into serving others. Helping them with their lives meant she was less caught up in her own, and her own suffering gave her the ability to help them with their suffering. Not having children also gave her more time for her faith.

Sue understands how hard it is for me sometimes to be around my siblings with their children. She says it's natural to feel that way and reminds me I don't need to be superwoman. She and I share a Christian faith, and she tells me she enjoys being with Jesus now and is no longer jealous of her siblings. Her life gave her an understanding that the small pleasures are the important ones, and that you can have a good marriage without having children. She says she sees herself in me. Her advice is to keep talking to God. She says he knows his plan for me and whenever I don't understand, I can trust him. I needn't let other people tell me how things should be and what will make me happy.

Wednesday 3 June, 2020
15:30
I'm starting to get twitchy. It's been a week and I've heard nothing more from breast clinic. I'm sitting in my office at the hospital and

my cancer is all I can think about. I can't stand this waiting any longer. I was so hopeful and upbeat last week when I gave notice of my sick leave. I will be working from home but not doing any clinical work from 15 June. You can't do clinical work when you're self-isolating, can you? Why haven't I been called to pre-op clinic yet?

15:35
I call the breast care nurses.

'Hello, this is Marisa Wray. I spoke to Mr T last week and he said he wanted to schedule my op for the end of June, as they think they may have found some invasive foci. I was expecting to have been called for my pre-op by now. I don't want to muck work around and I need to give them dates as soon as I can. I'm a doctor, you see, and they need to get someone to cover me. I have to give them as much notice as possible.'

'I'm sorry but we haven't yet been given the go-ahead for reconstructions. We will call you next week if we have any news.'

Noooooooo! This isn't happening! The plan has evaporated, poof! I don't know where to put myself. I go for a power walk around the hospital grounds to let off steam. I feel a complete fraud. I've told work that I will be self-isolating from 15 June. And now I don't know. What I do know is that I am no longer safe to be doing clinical work beyond that date and that I need to stop. I feel sick. How long will work put up with my being off sick without even having a surgery date?

Any day now, I'm told, but we don't know when. More waiting. How do you weigh up the risk of waiting, which may cause the cancer to spread, against the psychological harm of having a mastectomy without a reconstruction? This is the situation in which I, and innumerable other women with breast cancer, find ourselves. So many unknowns. Does 'possible invasive foci' mean definitely invasive, or only possibly invasive? The MRI report graded the scan as MRI5, which means malignant - not just suspicious for malignancy - so I can't afford to wait but I don't want to even contemplate having a mastectomy without a reconstruction. That would finish me off altogether. I feel awful for saying it - I realise this is a situation many other women have had to deal with. Am I selfish? Yes, probably, but I had a glimmer of hope last week and it's about to flicker out.

15:54
In desperation I turn to Cancer Chat again and find a thread where I feel right at home.

Breast reconstruction cancelled due to coronavirus

Hi,
I am also awaiting mastectomy with immediate implant reconstruction for DCIS. My diagnosis has taken months and months as it is a big area and I had to have multiple biopsies before they were satisfied that it was DCIS. Now they have done an MRI and think they may have found an invasive bit, so the goal posts keep moving. Very worrying as I've been in the dark since end of Feb. The department I am with had a meeting about restarting reconstructive surgery last week but have not yet been given the go-ahead to resume as it's 'not safe'. The surgeon called me last week to say that ideally, he'd like to operate on me at end of June. I spoke to them again today and they say they will update me next week. At the moment they are only booking operating lists for 15 days ahead so patients can self-isolate for 14 days prior. I imagine if you have been invited for blood tests, they are planning on operating about 2 weeks later. It may be different where you are though. Each NHS Trust seems to have a slightly different approach. It's the waiting and uncertainty which is doing my head in.
    I just spotted that you wrote this post on Monday so I hope you got some more clarity when you went for the blood test. Let me know how it goes. I am getting my treatment in B.
Regards,
Marisa

Monday 8 June, 2020

I feel so much better when I'm immersing myself in work. Clinical work is too stressful to be compatible with my state of mind at the moment but I can share ideas about medical education, via Zoom, with the psychiatry leads from the other UK medical schools. It's a rarity for me to attend - it's impractical to travel from Cumbria to London for a ninety-minute meeting. Today I'm joining from the comfort of my sofa and I have the added advantage of being able to turn my video off.

Later, I'm in my element explaining neurotransmission to medical students in a live Q&A session for some lectures I pre-recorded for them to watch at their leisure. It's such a relief when my thoughts are otherwise occupied.

12:00

I also have a remarkable meditation with Merryn.

I see a flower in a forest. Its delicate pink petals and deep-green spotted leaves unfold at the foot of a giant tree. It's the only one of its kind here and I want to sit and look at it. Had I been rushing I would have missed it. It's good to take the time to appreciate such beauty. Not all endeavours need to be uphill, hard and challenging. Slower pursuits can give as much pleasure. They allow me to look purposefully at the things that grab my attention. I am also reminded that looks can be deceptive. The flower is much stronger and hardier than it appears. It gets enough water and sunlight, and its beauty stops people from treading on it.

I see myself as a little girl, clambering over rocks on a beach in Jersey. Her beauty lies in her sense of adventure, fascination with life and willingness to explore. Next, I see my teenage self flying through the air, turning somersaults on a trampoline. It's the closest feeling she'll get to flying. Her beauty lies in her openness to new experiences. Now I see my adult self, more confident and still open to trying new things. Although she is less free, she considers others more. Her beauty lies in her goodwill, compassion and interest in others, and in her sense of humour. She wants to embrace and bless the people she meets.

I am suddenly aware that the flower cannot last forever. I wonder how it will cope with dying? I receive an answer: it will cope by remembering how beautiful it was. *On est bien peu de chose, et mon amie la rose, me l'a dit ce matin…* Thank you Françoise Hardy.

I am feeling hopeful. The dark forest is now infused with light. The cells in my breast remind me of what it means to be healthy. They're forcing me to slow down. To become softer, less hard-edged. To stop and smell the roses. To make them behave normally I must find and do the things that bring me joy, like walking in nature, painting, immersing myself in a good book, understanding new science, connecting with friends, contributing to community, and gaining knowledge in order to teach it.

Merryn says the flower represents me. It symbolises the beauty in me and in my life, and shows that my perceived weaknesses are indeed my strengths. The flower feels like an exceptional being. The only one of its kind.

Unknown to me, Merryn wrote a poem for me two weeks ago. In light of today's meditation, she sends it to me now.

Marisa's Poeme
Delicate flower of the palest pink,
Fragile, yet the beauty is held within,
Its fragility, its delicacy,
Therein its pure potency resides.
Oh, how it doth shine amongst the rest,
Beneath a canopy of forest green,
So frail, a thing of such rarity,
Poised, balanced upon a single stem.
Open, its face tilted to the sun,
A strand of light carefully lain,
Across the flush of its tender cheek,
Momentarily paused in time.
Drab uniformity of wooded clones,
Cast light upon its brilliance!
Its passionate intelligence!
Its natural divine perfection.

19:02
WhatsApp conversation with Amanda.

Hi Marisa, how's it going? Hope ur doing ok?

Head been ready to explode for a while so have taken decision to cease clinical work after this week. Not got date for surgery yet but hoping end of June. They still haven't had go-ahead for reconstructions though. Trying to stay calm! Are you having a good break? I'm about to do ukulele group via Zoom. xxx

Ah dude that sounds incredibly stressful. I'm sure you've made a good decision. Tho I'll be sorry not to see u next week.

I'm ok ta, feel like I've been away from hospital for ages, which is probably what I needed. Xx

Thursday 11 June, 2020

Yesterday we all queued up at work to get our COVID-19 serum antibody test. Today I manage to run an outpatient clinic over the telephone. Whilst eating my lunch, I amuse myself by learning about interpretation of MRI breast scans.

Thursday night is ASDA shop and stir-fry night. It goes badly. Steve and I are both so tense, we end up shouting at each other over nothing. I can't stand it any longer. Steve retreats to watch TV. I don't know what to do with myself. I need to get out. I feel desperate. My appetite has disappeared.

I pack a bag, grab a blow-up mattress and drive to the office. It's deserted. I frantically google how to fix things after you've walked out on an argument. The articles I read say don't walk out - you'll regret it! Great. I consider calling the Samaritans but think better of it. How could they help? I know I've done something foolish. I head back home.

Friday 12 June, 2020

Today is my last day at work and I'm pacing around my office, going berserk. My situation feels intolerable. I am a fraud. I don't deserve to go off sick. I don't even have a firm date for my op yet. What am I going to do?

As time has gone on, I have struggled more and more to make clinical decisions. All my patients are complex and there is a lot of emotional distress. This is multiplied when I can't see them face to face so have to make difficult decisions based on a telephone assessment. My usual clarity of thought is muddled and murky, and I'm worried I might harm someone inadvertently through indecision. I know I am making the right decision to stop clinical work, and this was legitimised by the surgeon on 27 May. I realise it's daft to feel I need to legitimise it but now the goalposts have moved again and I still don't have a date for my surgery. My team have been telling me for weeks that they're astounded I'm still managing to work at all. Why can I not afford myself the same mercy?

I can't sit still. I feel sick. I need to act. I call the Breast Cancer Now helpline. The woman I speak to gives me some practical advice. She sounds worried about me. Listens. Hears my distress. Takes me seriously. She suggests I email the breast care nurses.

13:54

From: Wray Marisa
To: breast care nurses
Subject: Appointment

Hello,

I don't mean to hassle as I know you must all be incredibly busy. I have been trying to phone but there is no answer and I have had no response to the message I left yesterday.

Mr T phoned me just over 2 weeks ago to say that he was hoping to schedule my surgery (mastectomy with immediate implant reconstruction) for the end of June. When I called for an update last week, I was told that the Trust has not yet given the go-ahead for reconstructions.

I have heard nothing this week but I just received a cryptic text to say that my appointment at 3.15pm on 17 June will be by telephone and not face to face. I was not aware that I was supposed to have an appointment on 17 June.

I know that I have to self-isolate for 14 days prior to surgery, so it is clear that my surgery will need to be at least 14 days later than 17 June at the earliest.

The waiting and uncertainty along with the feeling of disempowerment has taken a toll on my mental wellbeing and I am now signed off work sick after today (I am a doctor in the NHS). I was working on the basis that I would have to self-isolate for 2 weeks prior to 30th June, so work was expecting me to go off sick from next week anyway. My husband is also very unwell with anxiety and depression due to all the uncertainty and the effect of Covid (he is going to lose his job).

I would be so grateful if someone could let me know the nature of my appointment next week and whether there is likely to be a much longer wait for surgery than we anticipated 2 weeks ago when I spoke to Mr T.

Kind regards,
Marisa

14:50
My phone rings. It's the breast care nurse. She must be telepathic because she has not seen my email but apologises for the delays and says she feels hopeful they might get the go-ahead to resume reconstructions any day now. (Yeah, right.) The surgeon is well

aware of me and will call me next Wednesday to make a plan, one way or the other.

15:15
I text my church group leader.

> Hi Steph. Please can I make a very specific prayer request. My surgeon still has not had the go-ahead for reconstructive surgery. He wanted to operate at end of June as didn't want to risk leaving it any longer. I have phone appointment with him Weds next week. I will need to decide then whether to have mastectomy without reconstruction or wait indefinitely for mastectomy with immediate reconstruction. The psychological effects on me of not having reconstruction will be utterly devastating. But delaying might affect my survival. Please can we pray that he gets the go ahead for reconstructions next week. If not, I am not sure how I will cope. Steve is in an awful state, worse than me. Thank you. xxxxx

I can't bring myself to say goodbye to my team. I slope off with my tail between my legs. I think this may be the worst I have ever felt. Guilty at not being able to 'soldier on', desperate to find some clarity and a plan. What am I going to tell Steve about my inability to carry on working? Will I ever work again? Will we both be out of a job? Why on earth have some parts of the country restarted reconstructive surgery while others haven't? I have heard from a woman in Kent via the Cancer Chat forum that she had her mastectomy and immediate implant reconstruction a couple of weeks ago.

Mum texts to ask how I am. She responds to my plight by putting me in touch with a friend of my sister's whose father happens to be an eminent oncologist in London. To my amazement, the friend contacts him, sends me his number and tells me to FaceTime him in the morning. You can't say my family are not resourceful!

124

Saturday 13 June, 2020
08:26
I am FaceTiming the oncologist. He's in his dressing gown, having just got out of the shower. I'm so grateful to him for talking to me!

He says no one is happy with the state of cancer surgery at the moment, and the Trusts are all doing their best to resume reconstructive surgery. Some have made more progress than others. He does not advise moving my care elsewhere as the situation is much the same all over the country. He's hopeful that implant reconstructions will be among the first to restart. He suggests I go on tamoxifen if I'm worried in the meantime, as it will slow down any invasive cancer. He also says that compared to other cancer drugs it has negligible side effects.

10:00
Steve and I are on our way to visit his mum before I may have to start self-isolating. We stop for a petrol-station coffee. I feel embarrassed to be telling Steve's mum that I don't have a date yet but I've stopped work.

'Are you sure it was a good idea to stop work?' Steve asks.

I shudder. He's only concerned for my welfare, but I take it the wrong way. 'Don't put pressure on me!' I snap.

'I'm not putting pressure on you!' he insists. 'You've said how being at work takes your mind off things.'

I feel ashamed to no longer be working, especially as he quit his job a few weeks ago. We are both feeling the pressure.

Sunday 14 June, 2020
We walk for seven hours over the Coniston mountain range. How wonderful to be in nature. We both feel a little more relaxed.

Monday 15 June, 2020
I feel a palpable sense of relief from not having to think about clinical work. The tension between Steve and me has also dissipated. It was definitely the right decision. I try to hold the uncertainty as lightly as I can.

12:00

I have my ninth meditation with Merryn. We are meditating for so long that I end up with a numb bum!

Today, I am a fish, feeling safe and at home in a rockpool. In the human world, this is how I feel among mountain landscapes when I know where I am and where I want to go. It also feels playful and companionable to be part of a school of fish - just how I feel when I am with my girlfriends from church. We share a strong connection. I love how the school moves together and splits its time between the contained, warmer waters of the rockpools and the cool, unknown waters of the open sea.

We venture further out to sea and I become separated. I slow down and keep my senses peeled. I feel the currents around me and follow the warmest one. I feel at one with the water and grateful that I am designed to be able to do this. When I am lost on a hike, I also use my instincts. They tell me to make a mental map of where I have come from. I note the hills, rocks, streams and paths. I can sense where the sun should be and know roughly the direction I need to go in. It's nice to plan and be in control, but there also needs to be an element of the unknown - to create adventure.

I look back on my life path and see where I have come from. I can see that it has been an exciting and varied path – so many experiences. I am being shown this because it is easy to forget the places I've been and things I've done and to dismiss them.

'What have you given birth to here on Earth?' Merryn asks me.

'Hope to people when they felt they had no hope, laughter and encouragement,' I answer.

'It is also important to give this to yourself,' she says.

I can see that the path forward will take me on to adventure.

'What is your ultimate goal?'

'To have touched as many lives as possible,' I say without hesitation.

I realise I could not achieve this if I had children.

I am back in the rockpool, feeling content and enjoying the different colours and shapes of the seaweed and the way it waves.

Merryn says today's meditation is perfect confirmation that I am on the right path with everything I'm doing. Just as I trust my instincts, I have to trust that everything is exactly as it's meant to be.

Tuesday 16 June, 2020
15:00
My counsellor notices that I am visibly more relaxed than I have been in recent weeks. Another confirmation that I have done the right thing ceasing clinical work.

I don't let myself think about how long I might be in this limbo.

PART TWO
THE SUMMIT

Chapter 10

Glorious Self Isolation

Tuesday 16 June, 2020
17:30
My phone rings. It's the breast care nurse. Hang on, I was expecting a call from the surgeon tomorrow, not today.

'Are you able to start self-isolating from midnight tonight?' she asks.

Wow! 'Does that mean I have a date?'

'Yes, we have you booked in for surgery on the first of July.'

Yes! Yes, yes, yes! OK, what do I need to know... 'When will I have my pre-op?'

'We can do some of it by phone but you will have to go to Hospital B early next week to have bloods and a physical exam.'

'Won't that be breaking my self-isolation?'

'No, a visit to the hospital doesn't count.'

'Oh, OK. In that case, can I go out for a walk when no one is around?'

'No! That's not allowed!'

'Oh, right.' Strict isolation within the confines of the garden gate it is.

'You will need to have a Covid test forty-eight hours before your operation.'

'Do I need to do a two-and-a-half-hour round trip for that or can I have it done locally?'

'I will look into it for you but I hope so.'

'Thank you so much, I really appreciate it.'

Hurray! Action stations. I call out to Steve. Better get to ASDA to stock up for a fortnight!

18:09

Oh my gosh, I'm slightly hypomanic in the supermarket! What do I need for two weeks of self-isolation? Pasta! Tins of tuna. Some treats… hmm, let me see. I suddenly want to buy the whole shop.

19:17

I need to WhatsApp the world (well, family, Amanda and Louise) with the news and email my counsellor. This is so exciting - we only had a session a few hours ago when I was still in limbo.
I start to plan my fourteen days. I'm not sure when my pre-op will be - they keep sending me messages that contradict each other.

Wednesday 17 June, 2020
10:00

I'm beaming from ear to ear as I log on to Zoom to spend a few hours teaching GP registrars about dementia.
It's not as easy as teaching face to face, but we have fun and there are not too many attendees so I am able to answer all of their questions and make the session as interactive as possible. See? I can still work when I'm self-isolating!

16:00

I am empowering myself to face losing my breast. I feel strangely upbeat about it. By the end of the afternoon, I am as well informed as I can be about the ins and outs of pre-pectoral implant reconstructions, complication rates, what to expect when you go in for surgery, what to wear and so much more.

17:45

I order some front-fastening bras and easy button shirts, then set up an ASDA delivery for next week. What a rigmarole that is! Should be much easier next time now that my shopping list is saved. Somehow, I also find time to catch up on Medscape with how Alzheimer's care has changed during COVID-19.
    Steve and I have been very lucky that we haven't experienced true lockdown until now. We live in a rural area and have been

accessing our daily exercise from our front door. I have been running, swimming and hiking the entire time. I now start to empathise with those who have been confined within their four walls (thank God we at least have a garden!) for all these months.

For the next few days, I build an exercise regime into my routine. I download a knackering workout, fifteen minutes of high-intensity interval training, which I follow with twenty circuits of the garden, dressed in my sports crop top and shorts, and finish with half an hour of yoga with Adriene on YouTube. After two weeks of doing this daily I can almost do downward facing dog with my heels touching the floor – no small achievement since I have the tightest hamstrings in the world!

Thursday 18 June, 2020
14:33
Steve takes to Facebook and posts a picture of us from our March hiking trip.

> Pic from early March on the summit of Ben Macdui. The story behind the pic: we were on tenterhooks waiting for Marisa's breast cancer biopsy results. 15 weeks and a Covid lockdown (when the NHS became a Covid-only service) later, we finally have a date for surgery. They say the cancer is low-grade (DCIS) and unlikely to kill her any time soon, but that's easy to say when you're not the one with the large tumour growing in your breast! We are now in self isolation prior to the op for 14 days until 1st July.

> Anyone that knows me knows I tend to project a positive outlook and keep my feelings to myself but I don't mind admitting I'm finding things hard at the moment.

Many of Steve's friends had no idea what has been going on in our lives. The response is an outpouring of good wishes and understanding of how hard it must have been.

He doesn't share this with me at this point, but Steve is dreading what's to come - he doesn't know what to expect. What will I look like after my surgery? Will I be left with a flat scar and no boob on one side? He googles stories of men who couldn't cope with their wife's mastectomy and ended up divorced. Will he still fancy me or be able to look at my absent or deformed breast? He feels angry and questions whether a mastectomy is really necessary. Much later, when he shares these thoughts with me, he qualifies it by saying, 'I'm a normal male - I do like looking at boobs!'

Friday 19 June, 2020
I feel like writing a blog. I started bigholeblog a few years ago when I was processing my grief over being childless. I haven't written for a couple of years. Might as well start adding to it now. Unimaginatively I entitle my first post The C Word. While the C word is very rude in English, the French equivalent – *con* - is much less so, and I think we all agree that cancer in the time of coronavirus, *c'est con*!

Over the next few weeks, I will write about fifteen entries, chronicling my breast cancer journey. A bit corny, I know, but it is so cathartic.

Saturday 20 June, 2020
Who knew there would be so many jobs to do in the garden once I was confined within it!

Monday 22 June, 2020
14:00
I didn't realise a Zoom meeting could last for four hours. Oh my, what a marathon! Normally I thoroughly enjoy my jaunt to Warwick University to spend two days with colleagues from all over the country, vetting questions for the Medical Schools' Council exam bank. Today we are doing it remotely. Even with a coffee break in the middle, I have square eyes. It's surprising how

much we manage to achieve doing it this way. I miss the wonderful catering though.

Tuesday 23 June, 2020
I surprise myself by making the most delicious homemade hummus ever. It's lucky I'm self-isolating as I add double the amount of raw garlic.

Wednesday 24 June, 2020
08:00
It's time for another visit to Hospital B. This time it's to be measured for my implant. The breast clinic has moved to another building. It's very modern - much nicer than the other one.

09:30
The place is so quiet that I stand in front of a glass screen for five minutes before the receptionist, who is in deep concentration inspecting patient records, notices me.
'Sit over there please!' she instructs me in a mildly annoyed tone as if I should know this already.

09:45
I don't have to wait too long before I'm ushered into a clinic room. I'm told to undress my top half and don a very pretty, pale-pink cape which reaches my midriff.
I finally meet Mr T, with whom I've only spoken on the phone so far. He's very friendly and we have a chat and a laugh. He's leaving the NHS in a few weeks - I've only just caught him in time, phew! Work-life balance, he says - the NHS doesn't appreciate him. I have some sympathy. Good luck to him!
I stand bare-chested while he measures the distance between my nipples, from nipple to collar bone and inframammary crease. I have zero ptosis - not a droop in sight.
'Did you know that your left breast is bigger than your right?' he asks.

'It never used to be -it's been punctured so many times it's turned into a pincushion.'

'Oh, have we VABed you to death?'

Er, yup!

11:00

I'm starting to lose my patience a little. I'm having my pre-op assessment down the other end of the hospital. Poor Steve is waiting outside in the blistering sunshine and here I am, pacing up and down outside a locked door. I've rung the bell about fifteen times with no answer. I hammer on the door and someone eventually answers. 'Someone will fetch you soon.'

11:55

It's been nearly an hour now and no one has come. I must have done 1000 steps up and down the corridor! The arrival of another patient with an appointment later than mine prompts me to phone the pre-op number again.

'Hello, I'm running out of patience! I've been standing outside the door for an hour. They said they were expecting me but no one will let me in!'

12:15

Finally, I am weighed (60kg), measured (167cm - have I shrunk? I'm sure I'm 168!) and have bloods and blood pressure taken. All tickety-boo.

12:45

Last on the list is a consult with the breast-care nurse, who shows me some implants and gives me advice on bras. Wow, these implants are big and heavy!

'Mine will be smaller than this, won't they?' I'm surprised at how heavy a breast is. Oh well, as long as it matches the other side!

'Erm, how soon will I be able hike up mountains again after my op?' I ask her.

A look of horror appears on her face. 'You're having an implant reconstruction! You must take care of it! At least six weeks until you should do anything strenuous.'

I ask if she's had other patients who are runners. She tells me the last one they had waited twelve weeks before running again. I guess it will depend on how the implant beds in. She also tells me that I will have a drain protruding from my mid-axilla for two weeks after the op and won't be able to raise my arm more than ninety degrees. How lovely. I start to feel a little apprehensive.

Sunday 28 June, 2020
09:00
Covid swab time. After much telephoning to and fro, I eventually manage to negotiate having the swab taken at my nearest hospital, half an hour's drive away compared with one and a quarter to Hospital B. It's a bit uncomfortable but doesn't take a minute and I'm assured the results will come back before Tuesday.

11:58
I am having a distinct wobble. I find the blog written by Liz O'Riordan, a breast surgeon who was diagnosed with breast cancer herself and had a very tough time of it. I decide to email her.

From: Marisa Wray
To: Liz O'Riordan
Subject: Solidarity in breast cancer

Dear Liz,

I have been feeling the need to connect with other doctors who have been through breast cancer. I am having a mastectomy with immediate implant reconstruction in 3 days' time.

I have been reading your wonderful blog in order to prepare myself for what is in store for me. I'm having an immediate implant reconstruction (pre pectoral). I'm slim and very athletic (though not as slim as you!) and am dreading not being able to cycle, run, wild swim and climb mountains. I am also horrified about losing all my fitness. I am also grieving the impending loss of my athletic figure. How on earth did you cope with it all?

I also feel guilty about being off work. But I know that I have to prioritise my health. How soon did you return to work after your surgery? Were you able to? Anyway, I know that you must know how I feel and I wanted to touch base with another doctor who has been through this. I know you went through chemo as well so it sounds like you had to suffer far more than I have had to so far. The Covid wait has been like torture though, I have to say.

I'd love to hear from you if you are able to respond.

Best wishes,
Marisa

I don't receive a reply but it helps just to have sent the email. Liz's blog makes for a wonderful, if at times harrowing, read. Maybe now is not a good time for me to be reading it!

Monday 29 June, 2020
I distract myself by writing anatomy hotspot questions on brain circulation for the medical students. I also have my last meditation with Merryn.

12:00
I'm safe in the arms of Jesus. He tells me not to be afraid. 'Perfect love casts out fear,' he says. I can slow my breath and focus on Jesus's presence here with me. He knows what's going on in every cell of my body. His hand on my head is very warm and emits an

orange glow. I can surrender to putting myself in the expert hands of another [my breast surgeon]. I can trust and allow myself to be vulnerable. Instead of feeling scary, it can feel daring and exciting, like a new adventure. I can step into my operation willingly.

Jesus shows me the way down to the seabed. I'm lying there comfortably. I don't need to breathe. I look up and see the light dancing on the surface of the ocean. I feel cocooned and safe. Beauty is all around me in the fish, the coral and the fronds of seaweed. When the time is right, I have the overwhelming urge to crouch, prime my muscles and surge in one lithe movement up to the surface. My head breaks through the water and I take in a huge breath. I smile – I see that Jesus is everywhere, in everything, and it makes me feel safe.

Tuesday 30 June, 2020
09:00
I receive a text from Merryn

> **Wow!! AMAZING work yesterday Marisa** 🐚.
> **Remember that Jesus is everywhere and makes you feel safe and reassured. Call on him whenever you need him. I'll be with you in spirit when you go in for your surgery tomorrow. Trust and know that it will all be perfect and I look forward to hearing how you get on. LOADS of love and light being sent your way.**
> **Merryn xxx**

Thanks Merryn! I feel zen now.

12:35
I can't help myself. I am mourning the impending loss of my fitness and my ability to run and swim. When no one is looking I sneak out and go for a run and swim in the local river. Oh, the ecstasy! I really needed that. This is the best physical shape I've been in for years. I need to capture it for posterity. Today I need to feel my physicality.

Back at home in the shower, I let the needles of hot water massage my scalp and warm my skin. Liz's blog has given me the idea of taking some (tasteful) naked photos as a record of what I look like now - before the chop. Steve walks in and wonders what on earth I'm doing. He's overcome with sadness when he realises. He's always loved my nice, firm breasts! I don't feel sad as such. Just feel the need to mark my loss. Then move on.

Gotta be up at the crack of dawn tomorrow.

Chapter 11

My New Boob Is Numb

Wednesday 1 July, 2020
06:00
Have I got everything? Let's see, front-fastening bra, button-up top, zip-up fleece, tracksuit bottoms (all easy to get on and off), toothbrush, tiny tube of toothpaste, soap, lip salve (it's warm and dry in the hospital), phone, charger, book…

07:30
'Bye Love!'
Steve's not allowed into the hospital so I venture in alone. I'm glad I'm me rather than him at this point in time. I wonder what he'll do with himself for the next few hours?
I'm early. There's a security guard on the door to whom I show my letter. He asks me if I know where I'm going. I think so. I pick up a face mask and stride purposefully in the direction of the gynaecology ward. No, breast surgery is not a gynaecological procedure, but that's where I'm told to go. I walk in on the nurses' morning handover meeting.
'Er, sorry to butt in like this, but am I in the right place?' Apparently not. I'm supposed to be in the gynaecology and breast day surgery unit. Normally my procedure would be done as a day case but because I live so far away, Mr T wants me to stay overnight.
I turn on my heel and walk down deserted corridors to my destination. The door is locked and there's not a soul about. I ring the bell. No answer. I'm still very early so I amuse myself by walking up and down and doing deep knee bends to keep my circulation going. I don't think there's any CCTV here… I'd look very odd to any observer. I feel hungry but I'm not allowed to eat.

141

My last meal was at about seven last night. Always hungry. I can have a sip of water though.

I hear somebody moving around inside so I ring the doorbell again. This time a rather hassled-looking nurse opens it for me and apologises.

'Sorry, I was just in the changing room. You can't hear the bell from in there. There's only me here today.'

I smile. 'That's fine, I'm not in a hurry.'

08:30

I'm ushered into the day surgery unit. The beds have all been removed just in case coronavirus decides to take up residence here. It's so empty I can almost hear an echo. There is a lone green armchair in which I sit, a queen on her throne.

The nurse appraises my feet. 'What size TED stockings will you need?'

'Small. How many sizes do you have?'

'They go up to XXL, I think,' she says as she hands me a pair.

Green. Fetching. Well, better than the old-fashioned white ones. There's a hole in the toe so she can check my feet are not turning blue. I have to also don a gown, which can be removed with ease when I'm transferred to the operating table. I try not to think about it and instead ask the nurse about how things have been going. She tells me they've only just resumed operating lists and it's been a frustrating time. How many are on the list today? She doesn't know but she's not expecting anyone else here today. I have a whole unit to myself but I won't be here long. After my op, I will go to recovery then to the gynaecology ward onto which I stumbled earlier this morning.

08:45

There's a smile behind that mask. I'm straining to understand the jaunty anaesthetist who talks very fast with a distinct Dutch accent. 'You won't be sleeping as such, you know I'm going to be poisoning you, don't you!'

142

Face masks are now mandatory for anyone in hospital since the government, in its wisdom, decided fifteen weeks after coronavirus peaked that masks might reduce the spread of the virus. Masks are not only uncomfortable, give you spots and make your glasses steam up, but they make it so much harder to understand what the other person is saying. The words ketamine and morphine are clear enough, but I am really not in the mood for discussing the relative merits of tramadol and codeine (worst for constipation). Let's just go for morphine for post-op pain relief if that's what you normally use. Being a doctor-patient is always a tricky line to tread…

09:00
Mr T swoops in, full of purpose. The funny thing about surgeons is they're never happier than when they're cutting somebody up!

'Sorry about the list of possible complications,' he says, as I sign the consent form. The list is indeed as long as my arm.

'What's the risk of lymphoedema?'

'Four percent.'

Ugh, I don't want a swollen arm! 'What about infection?'

'I've lost two implants out of forty-two,' he says proudly. 'And those two had lots of risk factors.'

I don't smoke and I'm fit as a flea so I should be fine. I will have to keep a drain in for ten days. I mustn't let the district nurses remove it! And I must keep it dry.

A very chipper anaesthetic assistant comes to fetch me. There are a few more boxes to tick then we're off down the corridor to theatre, me padding alongside him in all my finery. We're a most cheerful pair. I'm in calm and inquisitive mode, taking in my surroundings. I don't think a hospital has ever been so quiet.

The friendly Dutchman reappears to put me to 'sleep'. I thank him for giving me a little pink cannula (I always used to put the bigger green ones in when I was a junior doctor).

'Did you think I was going to torture you any more than strictly necessary?' he kids, making me smile again.

I feel grateful. I was always a popular victim in the days when medical students were allowed to practice taking blood and putting cannulas in each other. I have great big veins, easy to palpate and a joy to cannulate. All good fun.

Next thing I know, a loud voice, which seems to come from far away, says 'We're just moving you into another bed.'

'That's fine…' I slur in reply without opening my eyes. I think that means I'm on the ward. I'm very groggy and more than a bit nauseated, otherwise it would be a rather pleasant feeling.

I pick up snippets of conversations going on around me as I doze. From the direction of the voices, I have worked out that I am in a four-bedded ward near the window. My opposite number is about to leave. From her words and the tone of her voice, I surmise that she's none too pleased about it but feels that she's not welcome to stay another night. I'm quite glad I'm still half asleep so I don't have to get involved.

15:00

I can't gauge the passage of time. It could be hours or it could be minutes until I'm sitting up and being offered a cup of tea. Hours, I think. Ugh, my throat really hurts. The anaesthetist did warn me about that. He said he'd use the least horrid airway but it still feels pretty horrid if you ask me. Every time I swallow, it feels as if I have globus hystericus, except it's real and not in my mind!

I'm starting to become a little bit more compos mentis. I take an interest in my two remaining ward companions. They both had laparoscopic hysterectomies the previous day and are staying one more night. They can't understand why the lady who left in a huff didn't just insist on staying one more night. It's not as if the ward is crowded.

16:30

I'm offered dinner but I don't feel remotely hungry so opt for a sandwich later. And several cups of tea. I call Steve, who is very relieved to hear from me seeing as he's been calling the ward since midday. He's been hit by a barrage of texts from my mum asking

144

for updates. Next, I call Mum to reassure her that all is well, then set to responding to a host of texts from friends and family. Wow, I'm popular!

I have a rather nifty contraption circling each of my calves: blow-up massagers which give my tight calf muscles a lovely squeeze every few seconds. I feel pleasantly drowsy and drop off for a bit. If it weren't for the nausea, which lasts a few days, I'd be quite keen on this general anaesthetic lark.

Mr T pops around to see me and admires his handiwork. It all went about as well as it could have gone, he tells me with a smile. He continues to smile as he tells me that tomorrow is his day off but another colleague will be in to check on me before I leave. He says my drain looks good - it's not draining too much - and I mustn't get it wet. It protrudes somewhere along my anterior axillary line near my eighth rib. I need to come back in ten days' time to have it removed. It's a very weird sensation.

I look down at my chest and gingerly touch the implant which feels cool under my skin. I mean, it's just under my skin. I have no fat in between my skin and the 'acellular dermal matrix', which is the pig skin holding the implant in place. The skin is totally numb. I know I've lost my nipple but I can't see my incision as it's covered by a very neat dressing. I try not to think about what it will look like when the dressing is removed.

Ooh, I need the loo. Having removed my calf massagers, I teeter towards the bathroom with a nervous nurse hovering at my shoulder in case I topple over. Woah, steady! They did offer me a bedpan but I thought I'd run the gauntlet, which I manage successfully. Not a bad effort for someone whose blood pressure was stubbornly refusing to go above 95/52 mmHg. I'm feeling very pleased with myself. Hope I don't need to go again too soon though!

I grin at my fellow occupants and introduce myself. They both have the same first name which makes it easier for me. I'm awful with names – they go in one ear and out the other. Before too long, the three of us are fast friends and having a good giggle. I learn how it feels to have your uterus removed via three holes in your abdomen and they learn about what it's like to wake up with a fake numb boob. I'm very chuffed that their consensus on my age when I arrived was about twenty-two - I'm forty-seven! My sisters and I inherited youthful genes from our mum, I think.

I feel slightly euphoric post anaesthetic, though still slightly nauseous. I can talk for England though and have fun with my co-conspirators until about nine when it feels like bedtime. I even make a surprise appearance at a Zoom meeting, which my group from church have been holding on a Wednesday night, and reply to a work-related email in which I mention that I've just come round from an anaesthetic and oh, the wonders of technology!

Thursday 2 July, 2020
I don't get much sleep because there is a chorus of snores (to which I'm probably contributing when I do sleep) and my chest is starting to ache - though the hospital bed is incredibly comfortable. At least the ward is cool and I can relax if not sleep. I become adept at removing and reinstating my leg massagers in order to make several trips to the toilet (at least I am well hydrated!).

02:00
I am convinced it must be morning as I feel wide awake.

07:00
Morning finally rolls around with yummy porridge for breakfast and copious cups of tea. I even manage to have a shallow bath, moving my rearranged body very gingerly, being careful not to get the drain wet. I forgot to bring a towel! Luckily the room is warmish and my now redundant hospital gown can double as a drying cloth.

I proudly slip on my front-fastening bra and button my baggy shirt over my tracksuit bottoms. Thank God for tracksuit bottoms. I am presentable and reasonably comfortable. Tying my hair back is a bit of a challenge because I can't raise my left arm to put it in a high ponytail like I usually do. Never mind, it will have to be a low ponytail - slightly skewed to the left.

Another surgeon comes to see me, as promised by Mr T who's on his day off. It turns out I'm famous around here because I'm the first reconstruction they've been able to do since COVID-19. Apparently they've been discussing my case every week, wondering when they would be able to whip the cancer out of my breast.

He tells me to come back in ten days' time for a post-op check and to have the drain removed, and to not be disappointed if my histology results aren't back for that appointment. Oh yes, I'm not out of the woods yet. They removed four lymph nodes, one of which was palpable.

He answers the worried look on my face by reassuring me that 'a palpable lymph node is neither here nor there'.

Really? Well, let's hope that the cancer is neither here nor there in my lymph nodes because I don't relish the thought of chemo or radiotherapy. Wouldn't it be nice if this was the end of it!

So that's it. He hands me a sheet of exercises to minimise muscle stiffness and ensure I regain my full range of movement without jeopardising the placement of my new implant. I just have to wait for my antibiotics then I am free to go.

Steve has arrived and gone for a coffee before driving round to meet me, and I'm already receiving messages asking whether I'm home yet. Normally mastectomy with immediate implant reconstruction is done as a day case, but Mr T wanted me to stay overnight because I live so far away. I have to say that I am glad of the extra care and the super-comfy hospital bed, along with the chance to check that everything still looks reasonable this morning. Every member of staff has been brilliant and the whole experience, if not enjoyable, was not unpleasant at all. Sometimes God seems to put people on your path to make things easier, such as my two co-conspirators who entertained me with such aplomb. I feel grateful for many things, not least my sense of humour.

Chapter 12

Front-Fastening Bra and Other Post-op Stories

Friday 3 July, 2020
Day two post-op
Its six in the morning and I'm wide awake, padding about the house in my pyjamas. I've worked out that if my top is loose enough, I can get it on over my head without having to raise my left arm much at all. Steve is incredulous. He usually gets up early and leaves me in the land of nod until at least eight, if I don't have to be up earlier for work. The thing is that sleeping with a breast implant and a drain stuck in your side is rather tricky and I wasn't prepared for night sweats.

Now, I'm no stranger to night sweats, having been going through perimenopause since failed IVF several years ago, but these were night sweats on steroids (and I'm not on steroids). I had no warning - I didn't even feel hot, I just woke up every ninety minutes drenched, pouring sweat and freezing cold. The whole thing was revolting. Not to mention uncomfortable in the extreme. After the third cycle, I stopped bothering to get up and change, having entangled myself in my drain each time I stumbled out of bed. I needed to pee every time, too. How could my body possibly be excreting so much fluid!

I'm going to have to do something about our sleeping arrangements. Steve gives out heat like a furnace at night and will insist on cuddling me (aw, and we've been married nearly ten years!) yet he doesn't sweat at all. Most unfair! I blame it on the duvet, on Steve's body heat and the fact my chest is a bit sore. No sign of infection though. I think a separate sheet and a thinner quilt are called for.

I establish a morning routine: gingerly swing legs over side of bed, careful not to pull at drain; orientate myself; slowly stand up; wait for foggy feeling to clear; walk to kitchen; take co-amoxiclav, ibuprofen and paracetamol combination; do arm exercises (congratulating myself for starting them as soon as I got home); run bath; perfect bathing position to achieve maximum soap coverage without getting wound or drain site wet (a bath pillow and flannel are essential items).

What a luxury to have a leisurely bath every morning! Steve comes in to check I haven't drowned. He's a picture of solicitude and is waiting on me hand and foot. Cup of tea? Why not!

I make myself comfortable on the sofa in the garden room and watch the rain. Rain is quite handy when you are day two post-op and don't feel up to doing much - at least I don't feel as though I'm missing out on any outdoor activities.

Steve supplies me with copious amounts of peppermint tea. I still feel slightly nauseous. I'm not sure whether to blame the anaesthetic or the antibiotics, or the fact that I'm eating too much because I feel ravenously hungry. Isn't it funny how you can experience nausea and hunger at the same time. I'm very relieved that I only need regular paracetamol and ibuprofen for pain. No opiates - I do hate being constipated! My day is punctuated by four-hourly intervals of taking antibiotics with breakfast, lunch and tea. Why, oh why is paracetamol so hard to swallow?

The breast care nurse rings to make sure Steve isn't about to drag me up Helvellyn mountain any time soon.

'Don't worry,' I tell her. 'Not this week or next.'

She gasps. I had her for a minute there! I promise that I won't try it for at least six weeks. I feel too wiped out to contemplate more than a walk round the block. I have less energy than I did yesterday when I managed a leisurely walk of about two kilometres. Maybe my body is trying to tell me something...

I don't much like my surgical drain, which protrudes from my armpit and necessitates that I carry a bag of bloody serous fluid (yuck!) around with me. It will be my constant companion for ten days. I'm grateful that my very trendy tote bag, which hangs from my shoulder, almost hides the tube which sticks out from under my shirt. The district nurse is coming every day to empty it. I guess I'd rather collect fluid in a bag than have it collect in my chest wall.

Saturday 4 July, 2020
Day three post-op
Having a separate sheet and light quilt makes little difference to my night sweats. Ugh! I google it and find several other women have experienced the same thing after an implant reconstruction. Strangely enough, it doesn't seem to feature with autologous reconstructions (using the patient's own body tissue and fat), so it must be something to do with the body's response to having a foreign object put inside it. At least I know it's not abnormal - I don't have a fever (I'm constantly on the lookout for infection) and most reports say it settles down after a few days.

The feeling of nausea hasn't quite gone, so I stay home while Steve goes into town. I feel a sudden need to socialise, so I join a Zoom cafe chat from the comfort of my sofa, where I'm super chirpy and talk a lot, then berate myself afterwards for monopolising the conversation. I guess I must be feeling a little better. I'm impatient for the district nurse to come and check on my drain because I'm dying to go out for a walk.

Steve and I make it as far as Hawes Bridge, the walk we normally do with Spook the cat in tow, which is about one kilometre each way. We bump into a neighbour who remarks how well I look: I always find such remarks rather disconcerting – is there a hidden meaning in that comment? Do they mean that they don't believe I've just had surgery for breast cancer? Are they just being polite? Are they insinuating that I'm well enough to go back to work next week? Am I paranoid or what!

Never have I appreciated the importance of a supportive bra as much as I do right now. Having always had small boobs requiring minimum support, I am discovering that most post-mastectomy, implant lingerie is made for women vastly more endowed than I am. Who knew that a front-fastening bra was a thing? I certainly didn't until the breast care nurse suggested I invest in one. Some of the brands are fiendishly expensive, but Amoena has a pale pink cotton one (ten percent Lycra so nice and stretchy) for under fifteen pounds, a worthy addition to my two post-mastectomy bras from ASDA, which look more like regular bras and fasten at the back. And it only took three days to arrive in the post.

I never thought I would find myself weighing up the pros and cons of bra options for holding a new boob implant. The front-fastening one definitely gives better support if going out for a walk or wishing to achieve a sporty look, or if you have to whip it off quickly for the surgeon to have a look at your wound. If you're just sitting around in it though, it can pinch a bit under the arm. The ASDA ones on the other hand are perfect for this: they are just like wearing a normal non-underwired bra with minimal support and are extremely comfy. They are also surprisingly easy to get on if you do up at the waist then slip the straps over your shoulders.

Sunday 5 July, 2020
Day four post-op
My bed covers were so light last night that I actually felt cold, yet I still woke up drenched. Not fun! No matter, I can always have an afternoon nap. Indeed, I need one daily at the moment. I don't sweat at all when I nap in the afternoon. How weird is that?

I have loads of energy this morning, so Steve and I decide to make the most of cafes being open again and walk to Old Sizergh Barn for brunch. It's one of our favourite places. If you time it right, you can watch the cows being milked from the comfort of the cafe, and the shop sells a variety of quirky gifts as well as organic vegetables. It's a forty-five minute brisk walk across the fields from our house but about fifteen minutes in, my new boob is feeling distinctly achy and it's pulling on my chest in the most uncomfortable fashion. I realise it was a mistake to wear my not-so-supportive ASDA bra and I end up walking with my hand underneath the implant, propping it up. Not a good look!

By the time we arrive, my ebullient energy has evaporated and I feel in serious need of a nap before embarking on the return journey. I hope a cup of tea and one of their cheese scones (to die for) will revive me, but I spend the afternoon sleeping for two and a half hours straight.

Monday 6 July, 2020
Day five post-op
Slight improvement in the night sweats, so maybe my body is starting to recover from the surgical insult and will settle down. I certainly hope so as I do love to sleep at night! Somehow, I've managed to overdo my activity two days running and have ended up in a stew. I'm convinced I'm getting lymphoedema - swelling of the arm due to lymph nodes being removed - as my armpit is a bit swollen and my left hand feels slightly puffy. I've never been good at pacing myself at the best of times, including the time I ran on a hamstring injury or broke my ankle showing off at the swimming pool. Let's hope it's just the result of having walked over 10,000 steps two days in a row. Time to apologise to my body and take it super easy for the next few days.

Tuesday 7 July, 2020
Day six post-op
Thank God, I don't seem to have lymphoedema. Phew! My drain is draining less every day, though it does seem a bit variable. Apparently this is normal. I give an interview to Paul from Cancer Care, a local cancer charity. It was through them that I accessed my counsellor, who continues to be a wonderful support. So that's it, my story's out - on the Cancer Care website!

I'm grabbed by the urge to share my story with whoever will listen to it. What's that about? Is it a need for recognition? I certainly recognise narcissistic tendencies in myself and an overwhelming need to be accepted, understood and approved of. On the other hand, I think my story is worth telling, and I can't keep it in. I am fast becoming a mad blogger.

Friday 10 July, 2020
Day nine post-op
It's time to have my drain removed. Yay! It's become a thorn in my side - no pun intended. The other day it started leaking because it was overly full and the district nurse, who hasn't come across one like mine, didn't know how to empty it. I ended up having to

wash my colourful tote bag because it got covered in bloody fluid. Lovely! Not one to be defeated by a leaky drain bag, I figured out how to open it and poured the contents down the sink myself. It felt so much lighter. The district nurses have been keeping a daily record of output, so it wasn't a problem to empty it. It has continued to leak though, so I have had to wrap it in kitchen towel to absorb the excess fluid. How delightful.

I was a little confused when the surgeon told me to come back to get my drain removed ten days after surgery, on July 10, having had my operation on July 1. Surely that's post-op day nine, not ten? The nursing journal authority says the day of surgery is day zero, so today is definitely day nine! Hmm, should I graduate onto the advanced arm exercises on Wednesday or Thursday? When exactly does the second week after the op begin? Minor, not to mention pedantic, concerns one might say, but this is the health of my new breast we are talking about. There are several threads on online forums discussing the very same subject. At least I'm not the only who is mathematically challenged!

No one seems too bothered in the clinic about what day post-op this is, and the surgeon (not Mr T, whom I will see next week) says it's fine that I'm still draining about fifty millilitres of fluid daily. The reason for having a drain post-op is to prevent the build-up of fluid, called a seroma. Seromas are quite common - they even run a seroma-draining clinic, which I hope I won't have to visit! With any luck this will be my penultimate visit to Hospital B. It doesn't hurt in the slightest to have my drain pulled out, and what a relief to walk around without it. I'm keeping my lovely tote bag, though.

The wound is looking tip-top, though not quite watertight yet (no wild swimming for me for a little while longer) and my first sight of it in all its glory is not as horrifying as I had feared. No nipple, but it's surprisingly well matched in shape and 'droop' to my real breast. I've acquired some new vocabulary recently, including the term 'ptosis' relating to breasts. As a medical student, I was familiar with the term in reference to eyelid droop, but until two weeks ago had no idea that the term could also be applied to how droopy your breasts are. I am the proud owner of two breasts with grade-zero ptosis.

It's still early when we leave the hospital and a beautiful day outside. Let's take the scenic route home! We wind our way through West Yorkshire, delighting in our slow passage past countryside and villages previously unknown to us. We find ourselves in more familiar territory once we reach Settle, where we stop at our favourite tea shop for lunch.

Shall we take a little stroll? I've no drain to drag around - I can move! It feels so good to raise my heart rate a little, feel my thigh muscles working and take some deep breaths. It's been ten days since I've done any aerobic exercise at all. I miss it.

Minutes later we're high above the town looking over the top of a precipice called Castleberg Rock. I had no idea this was here. On our way down some information boards tell us the Victorians built a pleasure park here together with fairground rides - I can just imagine it. As we descend through the undergrowth, we happen upon some climbers gearing up at the foot of the crag. It's a popular spot for local climbers. I smile ruefully as we engage in a bit of banter in climbing lingo. Those routes all look a little above my grade, even when I have full use of my left arm and pectoral muscles!

Saturday 11 July, 2020
Day ten post-op
I'm so thrilled to lose my drain that I suggest to Steve it would be fun to go for a 'little mountain stroll' to Potter Tarn. Encouraged by yesterday's mini excursion, I feel so great and full of energy. Bring it on!

Although it's nothing like our usual - only eight kilometres and 237 metres of height gain - by the time we get back down to Staveley, I'm ready to drop. Oh dear, my new boob has grown by about thirty percent and it feels uncomfortably tight. Have I overdone it? I did wonder whether I was at risk of seroma as my drain was still draining about fifty millilitres when they took it out, but I'm told that is normal. The trouble is, I've never experienced anything like this before so how do I know what is normal and what isn't? The skin over the implant feels decidedly warm to the touch but no redness, which would indicate infection.

Sunday 12 July, 2020
Day eleven post-op

Sweat, sweat, sweat. Oh no, it's the middle of the night and I'm lying awake, freezing cold and soaking wet, wondering whether my boob will inflate to a double G cup by morning.

I awake at seven. That was a long night! I gingerly feel my boob. Thankfully it hasn't grown any bigger. I feel a wave of relief. A few text messages later and I am under strict instructions from my old medical school friend to 'lie down flat for a couple of hours morning, afternoon and evening'.

'Think of a sprained, swollen ankle,' she advises. 'And no more "mountain strolls"!'

Yes, doctor!

I turn all philosophical and write a blog post.

Creating joy

I have always loved the title of CS Lewis' book *Surprised by Joy*, chronicling his spiritual journey into Christian faith, and it is no coincidence that he married Joy Gresham two years after she edited the book's final draft. The anguish Lewis felt over her death speaks into the human experience of suffering. It seems to me that joy and pain are inextricably linked, and as I have grappled with my experience of involuntary childlessness and then cancer, I have at times found my thoughts running parallel with Lewis' heart-wrenching lament in *A Grief Observed*: 'The conclusion I dread is not "So there's no God after all," but "So this is what God's really like. Deceive yourself no longer."'

I stubbornly refuse to believe that God deliberately wants to cause us harm, be it emotional or physical, and have fallen on my 'God-given' gifts to ask myself what gives me joy? Can I create joy? I am unable to experience it in the smile of my own son or daughter or in a body which is entirely whole. And yet… And yet…

Painting

I always believed I was terrible at art. I never received more than a C in the subject at school, although I adored art history, especially since I learned that Van Gogh and I share a birthday. Something about Helen Segal, artist and fellow member of the online community of childless women to which I belong, enticed me to sign up to her 'Create Joy' course in November 2019 (https://empoweredchildlessness.com). I haven't looked back since. We created a 'cosmic smash book' journal full of JOY and pain. The process of creating it was truly joyous and extremely cathartic. I astonished myself by how much I loved every minute I was creating my own 'art', revelling in experimenting with colour, texture and form. I 'graduated' to learning how to paint watercolour and am now receiving commissions from family members and friends.

Making handbags

Part of my self-appointed occupational therapy while I was off sick from work a few years ago was to dust off my mother's old sewing machine and buy myself a book called *The Bag-Making Bible*. I ended up founding a business making and selling handbags! The creative process gave me real joy, as did the finished product. Sadly, I discovered there was no money to be made whatsoever in handbags, although I was extremely flattered when my niece, who had learned the new word 'rival' at school, said: 'Mummy, Cath Kidston is Auntie Misa's rival!' I still have some beautiful and expertly made bags for sale if anyone is interested…

Mountaintop experiences

I never feel better than when I'm climbing a mountain - the sheer physicality of it: my breathing coming fast, a sweat forming, my legs burning yet strong, the wind rushing past as I turn another corner where a new scene surprises me. My senses are sharpened, and I can eat as much chocolate and as many flapjacks as I like and still not get fat! I can't get enough of mountain adventures. And it's not just the mountaintop experiences that matter. The path up and down is full of interest, and the walk through a meandering valley has its own adventures.

Wild swimming

There's something about the sensation of being immersed in freezing cold water that invigorates like nothing else. I am totally addicted! I have a little 'jog swim' I do from home which incorporates a 15-minute run to and from the river with a 10-minute swim. It helps that I am warm enough when I get to the river to relish jumping in, and I have just about restored my core temperature by the time I get home! I am itching for my surgery wound to heal so I can feed my addiction once again. I seize every opportunity I have to swim in rivers or lakes, and especially in mountain tarns. The zing it brings is truly wonderful!

Elegant science

My chemistry teacher at school once remarked on my insatiable intellectual curiosity. I still have it. I remember tears coming to my eyes when I first read about the DNA triple helix and the mechanism by which the base pairs spell out a whole life. My breath caught and I marvelled at the simplicity and the beauty of it. I always have a need to understand how things work and fit together - to see the big picture. The joy I feel when I understand something new fills me with such excitement. I took it as far as a PhD, some of the best years of my life. I'm not sure I pushed any scientific frontiers but darn, I was an expert on dopamine neurotransmission in the rat brain!

Mentoring medical students
I fell into teaching almost by accident, but it is such fun! I often doubt that I am a good teacher but at least that means I am always striving to improve. I love the thrill of guiding someone to a new skill or understanding, that moment when their jaw drops and they say 'Ah, now I understand!' I like to think that I am growing the doctors of the future.

Ukulele
I had no idea when my husband booked us on The Big Acoustic Walk at Plas y Brenin outdoor centre in Wales a few years ago that it would inspire me to learn to play the ukulele. I'm terrible at it but after I joined a local strumming group, The Bryce Street Strummers, I learned that my degree of talent mattered not one jot, as I could strum along to my heart's content with a bunch of friendly people who were having a whale of a time! They also say that learning a musical instrument is protective against dementia. What's not to like?

Novel cure
It is a gift to be able to enter someone else's world so entirely as to almost cease to exist oneself. I discovered that I could do this as soon as I picked up a story book to read to myself as a child. I am a slow reader but oh, do I savour every word. I take solace in the fact that until I lose my faculties or am no longer able to see or hear, that I will be able to vicariously experience the fullness of life.

These are just a few of the things that bring me joy. I could add yoga and meditation to the list, as well as spending time

with each of my seven nieces and nephews. Oh, and eating!
A delicious meal with a glass of wine always goes down well.

At the end of such a productive day I decide to amuse myself by
drinking gin and eating the strawberries I picked from the garden
this afternoon.

Chapter 13

Wound Healing Shenanigans

Wednesday 15 July, 2020
Day fourteen post-op
Today is my last visit to Hospital B. Mr T is super pleased with his handiwork. My wound is healing beautifully and there is only a minimum of swelling. I'm afraid the full histology is not back yet, but there was some invasive disease in there after all.

'Oh, so what does that mean?'

'You're supposed to take tamoxifen for five years. It improves your survival by about one percent or something. You might not like the side effects though, so do some research, see how you go, and decide whether you think it's worth it for you. Here's a prescription. You can pick it up at the hospital pharmacy. You get free prescriptions, but you'll have to pay for this one as you need to fill in the form via your GP.'

So that's it. I'm pronounced cured and sent on my way. 'Hang on, what if my lymph nodes are positive or the margins aren't clear?'

Pause. 'Well, in that case we're dealing with a totally different scenario. Radio and possibly chemotherapy. But don't worry, the chances of that are almost nil.'

I try to feel reassured.

Friday 17 July, 2020
Day sixteen post op
Steve has finally plucked up the courage to let me show him my wound and he agrees that it's not as gruesome as he feared. He really didn't want to have to look at it, but thankfully he still fancies me!

I've graduated onto the advanced arm exercises and it's all going swimmingly well. I can now raise my arm higher than ninety degrees and it feels tight rather than painful. Also, I'm no longer taking regular painkillers. I start taking pictures of my wound to chart the healing process. All is good.

I fancy going raspberry picking. There is a phenomenal crop lining the road over the Helm, just begging to be picked and eaten by Steve and me, but they're just out of reach. I wonder if I can get to them if I just stand on my tippy toes and lean forward a bit… Oops! I succeed in launching myself into the bushes and showering myself in raspberry juice. I land in the thorns with a bump. Oh dear, I can't hide the evidence. I look as though I've murdered someone. My shirt is covered in red splotches. Never mind, my boob is still intact. Unfortunately, the raspberries are swarming with tiny beasties, which decide to feast on the juicy skin just under the submammary crease of my new implant. Typical! Within a couple of days, it will itch like mad and be swollen and red but right now, I'm feeling rather marvellous and it's all a bit hilarious. Nothing will dampen my spirits. My parents are arriving on the train later and I'm so excited to be seeing them for the first time since Christmas.

Social distancing goes out the window as I can't resist giving Mum lots of hugs. I've got antibodies, and she has been very careful with her hand hygiene and wears a mask whenever she is out - I think the risk is low. Mum and Dad were a bit disconcerted by a passenger on the train who wasn't wearing a mask but felt it would be rather awkward to point it out to him. Who knows what his reasons for exemption were?

Saturday 18 July, 2020
Day seventeen post-op
I wake up to the smell of toast wafting from the kitchen. Dad must be up - he likes toast for breakfast. I can't do anything until I've had my daily porridge. My parents always sleep well when they're here - it's so much quieter than London… something soporific in the air.

What shall we do today? I'm feeling bright eyed and bushy tailed. We have a leisurely coffee stop at a new cafe in

Windermere, which makes a flat white to die for. We're greeted at the door by hand sanitiser and a contact-tracing form.

Afterwards, we head to Rydal Hall - a Christian retreat centre in the heart of the Lakes. The grounds are, on the one hand, well-tended enough to sport a croquet lawn and, on the other, wild enough to explore all day at our leisure. We go for the wild option. I can't believe we've never discovered the waterfalls walk at Rydal before. It's uphill and muddy but nothing my septuagenarian (you wouldn't know it) parents can't manage, and sufficiently attenuated for my healing body. The trail is peppered with sculptures, some made from scrap metal and others knitted into intricate patterns and shapes with great strands of multicoloured wool. I would normally refer to the walk as an easy stroll. What a find! Gushing torrents of water rush through a lush forest, hiding a hydroelectric scheme which powers the Hall. I'm dying to take a dip but must content myself with scrambling down (much to Steve's horror) to achieve the greatest proximity to the water short of immersion.

A little treehouse on the way down looks like a fun place for our packed lunch. Maybe not. Once we are squashed inside like sardines, we can't move our elbows! The picnic bench below proves a much better option. Had it been raining we'd have sought shelter inside The Grot, a tiny stone-built, wood- panelled room at the foot of the waterfall below the bridge, a Victorian whimsy which remains a hideaway for walkers and artists to this day.

As I contemplate the drive home, I realise that I'm not feeling too clever. I ask Steve if he wouldn't mind driving. I think I might have bitten off more than I can chew. On the way home, we pause in Ambleside for tea and gargantuan slices of delicious cake at a cafe we've not noticed before, in the hope that it might revive me. Mum and I share the last remaining piece of carrot cake and Steve has lemon meringue pie. Every time he eats lemon meringue pie he regales me with tales of his grandmother, whose lemon meringue pie was legendary. No other will ever quite live up to it!

By the time we arrive home, I'm feeling decidedly uncomfortable. I scurry to the bedroom and conduct a quick wound survey. Hmm, my new boob is throbbing, swollen and rather hot, and I really don't like the way the wound is looking. Oh no, what have I done?

'Love, I think I need to go up to the Urgent Treatment Centre to have it looked at,' I tell Steve.

I apologise to my parents for having to abandon them, drag myself back to the car and allow Steve to whisk me up to the local hospital. He has to wait in the car as only patients are allowed in.

My hopes do a little leap as I'm ushered into a room within five minutes, but it turns out to be the triage nurse. I return to the waiting room and make myself comfortable. By the time I'm seen, Steve has done several circuits on foot of the hospital grounds, discovered the location of the mortuary (hoping I wouldn't need it any time soon) and spent some time sunbathing on a bench.

The doctor agrees the wound looks infected. They take a swab, give me a new course of antibiotics and a nurse generously supplies me with adhesive dressings to cover the wound. I didn't think I'd be needing any more, but that was a bit optimistic. Sigh!

I'm really worried now. Have I jeopardised my implant in my enthusiasm to explore the outdoors? And the tiredness I feel is something else. I'm absolutely whacked!

Sunday 19 July, 2020
Day eighteen post-op
I feel like I'm walking through treacle. We take my parents out for lunch in one of our favourite pubs in Kirkby Lonsdale. We're about to order pudding when I renounce the idea in favour of returning home for an afternoon nap. I apologise for being a rather poor hostess. Time to send a picture to my breast surgeon friend. She quickly replies.

Ok... so your wound is red and at risk of opening up, which would be a problem as the implant is underneath. You need to take the antibiotics and lay flat for most of

the day, which will stop the implant from putting pressure on the back of the wound and give the wound a chance. You need to go and see the surgeon tomorrow morning and show him. Keep eating and drinking well of course. Fancy getting a mozzie bite too! Xxx

Spending the weekend lying on my back wasn't exactly what I'd envisaged for my parents' visit, but I think they understand.

The sun is still shining so Steve takes them for a walk along the river while I have a nap. By the time they return, I feel a little revived. Mum has been designing three-ply cotton face masks by drawing round a plate and reveals the secret of her pattern. I have some suitable fabric left over from my bag-making days so I make a mask with bumblebees on motorbikes for me (my favourite print!) and one with campervans for Steve – we had to sell our campervan, which we really miss. Mum and I sit companionably in the garden and stitch our way through to family Zoom time at six. Everyone is a bit alarmed by my wound woes, but I try to play it down. I leave a message for the breast care nurses to ask if I can come in and see someone tomorrow.

Monday 20th July, 2020
Day nineteen post-op
With my parents safely on the train, we're back off to Hospital B to have my wound checked. I am pleasantly surprised by the alacrity with which the breast care nurse invites me to come over today. I've been reading too many horror stories about implant loss due to the implant popping out of the wound (it happens with alarming frequency, especially if you don't have much fat), or wound infection. There are all sorts of horrendous wound infections. There is even such a thing as a latent - or late wound – infection, which lurks silently until several months after the op. Just when you think it's safe to get back in the water… bam! The entire implant is infected and is rarely salvaged at that point. These disasters play in my head during the long drive to the hospital.

The nurse gives me a stern look. Have I been climbing Helvellyn? No! Only a stroll up the waterfalls at Rydal. She doesn't think the wound looks infected but tells me to finish the course of antibiotics just in case. She agrees that it's looking a bit red and angry, and the implant is putting pressure on it. I need to take it easy to give the edges of the wound a chance to heal by primary intention. No one wants a lot of granulation tissue to form as the healing process takes far longer and the cosmetic result is inferior.

Over the next few days, I take serial pictures of my wound to chart its healing progress. I have to laugh because a few weeks later, I want to print some photos from my phone. The only way to select the ones I want is to display all of my photos on the screen of the machine in ASDA. There's no way of hiding the ones I'd rather not reveal to the world. I look on in horror as my breasts are displayed for all to see. I scroll down as rapidly as I can until the offending pictures are hidden. Not what I had in mind! Don't you love technology.

Thursday 23 July, 2020
Day twenty-two post-op
I've become slightly obsessed with photographing my wound and after two weeks, Steve suggests I take a weekly rather than a daily photo. OK! My pictures chart what a wound looks like when you overdo it, and how it improves when you lie down a lot and take it easy. Not easy to do for the likes of me. I write a blog post which I entitle 'Not for the Squeamish' in the hope of putting off readers who might not be able to cope with pictures of wounds (you can't really tell it's a breast from the pictures - they are not X-rated).

Oh, and I finally receive some good news - my lymph nodes and margins are clear. Whoopee!

165

PART THREE
COMING DOWN

Chapter 14

Survivor's Guilt

Monday 27 July, 2020
Day twenty-six post-op
I have too much time to think. Oh crikey, I need to prepare myself for going back to work! My original 'fit note' was only for eight weeks, starting on 15 June. I've never been very good at being off sick. Even though I was officially signed off work during my two weeks of self-isolation, I was still working from home. It's a funny thing with sick/fit notes. My long-term mental illness means sometimes I am not capable of full work duties. However, throughout my working life there has always been a dichotomy of sick versus well. There is no allowance to be fit for some duties but not for others.

I got into trouble as a junior doctor when my depressive illness got the better of me one morning and I had to go off sick. I was on call that night and my colleague, who oversaw the rota, begged me to work because they couldn't find anyone else to cover. Surely I was feeling a bit better now I'd had the day off? I decided that I was safe to work that night and I didn't want to let my colleagues down. I felt guilty for being off sick with depression, which was just a lack of moral fibre on my part, wasn't it? I wasn't so depressed that I was a danger to myself or my patients for this one shift. I just wasn't well enough to be at work full time. A colleague from medical staffing later explained that you can't work when you are off sick. But it's not that straight forward, is it? Just another example of presenteeism in a doctor.

So, I find myself stressing about going back to work. I have a telephone appointment with my GP. To my utter amazement, he agrees that my fit note needs to be extended beyond 9 August. I suggest he issues me with another note to cover until the end of August, which means I will return to work on 1 September. To me it feels a bit cheeky to ask for so much more time off but he is worried that September may even be too soon. I'm so glad I'm not my own GP! I gratefully accept this kind offer and think maybe I need to cut myself a bit of slack? Or maybe not...

I pick up a pen and start writing in my journal.

Apparently I have survived cancer. I'm not sure I even qualify as a cancer survivor. My invasive breast tumour was only Grade 1 and a few millimetres in size, hiding in a huge labyrinth of DCIS. I have read books and blogs written by 'survivors' who have endured so much more pain and suffering than I have. I only needed a mastectomy and have now been declared cancer-free without the need for either chemo or radiotherapy. I feel a bit of a fraud. I detect a large dose of imposter syndrome here. It's as if I am not worthy to be called a cancer survivor because I didn't have to go through as much hell as some others have. What am I complaining about? I'm not dead! The cancer didn't kill me like it has others. Ah, complex guilt.

It pains me to say this but why, as humans, do we always compare our own plight to that of others? There will always be people both better and worse off than me. Fact.

I feel anhedonic, tired, lacking in energy, unmotivated. Glum. Can't be bothered. Where did my mojo go?

Wednesday 29 July, 2020
Day twenty-eight post-op
I am cancer free. I should be rejoicing. Why am I in a funk? Since I received the all-clear (lymph nodes and margins) a week ago, I have experienced all sorts of emotions but none of them joyful. Why on earth don't I feel joyful? The truth is, there are many reasons - multifactorial aetiology as I would say to my students. Now, don't get me wrong, I am very glad that I am cancer-free and very grateful to have received the care and treatment I did. No more mileage-accruing trips to the hospital, biopsy needles,

anxious waits for results, second guessing when surgery will resume (COVID-19 has a lot to answer for), nor frantically seeking solace in online forums and helplines. But in their place, I am left with a void. Everyone thinks I am well but I am not. My wound is still healing, my sleep is poor and I still need an afternoon nap. Lassitude is my companion. Turning to the internet to try to find what's ailing me, I discover that these feelings are common. I have self-diagnosed survivor's guilt, 'life after cancer' syndrome (my term), and post-surgery fatigue.

Survivor's guilt is a well-recognised phenomenon in response to having 'survived' an event which other people have not. Why have I survived when others far worthier than me have died? Someone pointed out to me that from day one of being diagnosed with cancer you are a 'cancer survivor'. In medical terms, that makes sense as we talk in terms of survival curves, where percentage survival is plotted against time (as the years go by, the line on the graph edges down as people start to die). But a graph does little to explain what survivor's guilt feels like.

I'm cancer free! What's not to like? I can get back to normal life. Hang on. What is normal life? Is it even possible to get back to 'normal'? I think not. Yes, I can gradually resume activities I used to do before I had cancer, but I am forever changed physically and emotionally. I have lost a part of myself, and I have gained an implant, a scar and some pig skin. I have to take tamoxifen every day, a constant reminder that the cancer might come back in my other breast. Not that that worries me just now, but the knowledge of the increased risk will always be there. I'm in the limbo of having been discharged from breast clinic but not healed enough (physically or emotionally) to go back to work or do any of the sports that keep my mood buoyant. The skin that is stretched over my wound is tight and red, and my pectoral muscle keeps twinging. I hope that's normal. I feel guilty that I don't feel well enough to go back to work yet, even though everyone keeps telling me how well I look. I worry about my energy levels and whether doing this or that will cause wound dehiscence, a seroma or a late infection of the implant (my literature search tells me that this is common from six weeks to one year after surgery). Maybe I think too much.

Chapter 15

A Glimpse of Sunshine

Thursday 30 July, 2020
Day twenty-nine post-op
Tomorrow is Steve's birthday. We've treated ourselves to two nights in a B&B in Keswick. It's a chance to relax somewhere away from home, and test my legs and my wound to see whether I might be able to cope with a proper holiday in a couple of weeks. I'm so excited!

We love Keswick! As soon as we arrive, we make a beeline for our favourite cafe, Java, on the main pedestrian street. Restrictions have now been lifted so we can sit inside (the weather's a bit damp) and enjoy a flat white at our leisure. The sofas are taken (worst luck) so we settle for a bench but we're happy. I love the decor in this cafe. Their wall displays my favourite notice: 'Unaccompanied children will be given espresso and a free kitten'. Cracks me up every time. Then there's the framed letter displayed outside the toilet (where I have queued many a time), showing a grandfather apologising profusely for his grandson's inadvertent theft of the cafe's Trivial Pursuit cards, which form a little pile on each table to amuse us all. Takes me right back to the 1980s.

A leisurely stroll along the shore of Derwent Water is about all I can manage (let alone Catbells, Keswick's most popular mountain) and we finish the day with fish and chips, sitting on the edge of a cricket pitch watching the match as the sun finally emerges. Steve's idea of heaven!

Friday 31 July, 2020
Day thirty post-op
Heatwave. I suspect the usual tourist haunts, especially those involving a lake, will be heaving today so we head off to a lesser-known lake, Loweswater. The twenty-minute drive is worth it as

we barely see a person all day. I'm so tempted to go for a swim but I rein myself in and respect my wound, which is not quite watertight yet. The lake is the perfect size for someone who is regaining their fitness after surgery to circumnavigate on foot, and offers a beautiful spot for a picnic by the water's edge. Before lunch I go in for a paddle (only up to my knees). Ahh, bliss - cool water! There are some little kids nearby playing in a beached, disused dingy. Such adventures they are having - it's a joy to see.

By three, I'm in need of an afternoon nap. I still need one most days, especially if I've been out for a walk. And in this heat! Trouble is that the guesthouse doesn't open until five. There's a bench in the front garden so I opt to sit on it while Steve has a mosey around town. A phone message comes through from my colleague at work asking me to call her if I can. Hmm, she left it at ten this morning. That's a bit odd. I start to worry about what it might be. Better call her or I'll be stewing until Monday. When I eventually manage to get through, she sounds cheerful enough.

'Oh, it was just to find out when you're likely to be coming back to work,' she says.

OK, no drama. 'How about the first week in September?' I suggest.

'Oh, that's great!'

Not sure what that was about. The following week I find out that the Trust's legal team were trying to get hold of me. I've been subject to an investigation for a misdiagnosis which I made a few years ago. It was an honest mistake based on the information I had at the time.

In hindsight, I'm very grateful to my colleague for not spoiling my mini break.

Monday 3 August, 2020
Five weeks post-op
I must be the last person to finally have my hair cut after lockdown has finished! Ah, that feels better.

Tuesday 4 August, 2020

In a few days' time, we'll be off on a road trip around Northumberland and southern Scotland. Yay! I'm feeling a little more positive than I was last week. I've written two blog posts in two days. My fingers are on fire!

Musings from my sofa

There's nothing like enforced down time to make you take stock and consider what's important to you. Cancer does that to a person. I can't say that I'm glad this happened to me, but I have to take heart from some of the more positive outcomes. Maybe I think too much, but lately I've been mulling over what is important to me in life and mentally charting the course I took to arrive where I am now. I have absolutely no desire whatsoever to relive my more formative years (especially adolescence!) but I do owe some of my passion for life to the teachers and mentors who grabbed my attention and ignited my imagination.

Thank you Miss Dampier

I was an angst-ridden teenager and school wasn't exactly my favourite place. My English teacher came to the rescue (she explained to me on one occasion that she is a 'rescuer') and thank God she did, as her help, compassion, reassurance and guidance enabled me to swim rather than sink. I often felt like the man in the Stevie Smith poem, 'Not Waving but Drowning', though I was never the waving type so I think I might have just drowned quietly! Somehow, I managed to get hold of poor Miss Dampier's phone number and would call the unsuspecting woman late at night to pour out all my teenage angst into her very patient ear. Teachers are much maligned, but this remarkable woman did much more than just offer me succour when I needed it.

Thanks to Miss Dampier, I delved into Thomas Hardy's poetry, empathised with Mr Gradgrind from Dickens' *Hard Times* (didn't you love writing those empathetic essays for

GCSE English – in this one I was the remorseful Mr Gradgrind expressing his chagrin to his daughter with characteristic abandon!), learned Wilfred Owen's poems off by heart, and became *To Kill a Mockingbird's* number one fan. Jill Dampier and I are still in Christmas card contact, and she periodically updates me with news of others who touched my life through school. One such person is Mrs Sherratt, my brilliant biology teacher, who taught me how to write Oxford Entrance Exam-style essays in response to questions like 'Ladybirds are red. So are strawberries. Why?'

The periodic table
The person to whom I owe my love of chemistry is another teacher, now a friend, whose enthusiasm for the subject and inspirational teaching style made me hang on her every word. Dr Warwick thought I was rather gifted, too. My mother remembers her gushing at a parents evening, 'Marisa knows the answer even before I've asked the question!' I remember Dr Warwick chanting: 'electrolyse before our eyes!' and 'dehydrate, it is your fate!' during demonstrations of such processes. Now, many people find inorganic chemistry rather inert, but I just loved it. So did Primo Levi (I do seem to keep mentioning him), another hero of mine.

Manic rats in Oxford
My medical career has been somewhat circuitous but I can't say that I regret any of the odd turns it has taken over the years. From giving ecstasy to rats as a second-year medical student (my fascination with pharmacology began then) to returning to Trevor Sharp's lab in Oxford in between junior doctor jobs to do a PhD (this time the drug of choice was amphetamine to create an animal model of mania), then on to old-age psychiatry and more recently, branching out into medical education. I can't stop learning and I want to pass on that knowledge to others.

Having breast cancer has brought me back to my anatomy textbooks and performing PubMed searches for terms such as 'cutaneous innervation breast' and 'tamoxifen mechanism of action', which would never have crossed my mind as an old-age psychiatrist. Furthermore, I am now acutely aware of what it feels like to be a patient waiting for results, a diagnosis or treatment. And I have rediscovered my love of writing!

Chapter 16

Holiday!

Saturday 8 August, 2020
Five weeks post-op
I'm thrilled to be setting off on our first holiday since my cancer diagnosis. Normally at this time of year we go hiking in Austria but with coronavirus and cancer somewhat cramping our style, we've settled for a road trip around Northumberland and southern Scotland. A road trip has never really appealed to me before but given that I'm not up to climbing mountains, this is the perfect opportunity for a holiday that otherwise wouldn't even get a look in. Plus Northumberland has been on my list of places to go for far too long and while it's almost unheard of to be able to find a place to stay in Edinburgh in August, this year the Festival has been cancelled - another casualty of coronavirus. So this is our chance. Why not make it a loop and come home via Stirling? I've always fancied stopping off there. Stirling Castle punctuates our passage up the M9 every year on our way to the Cairngorms for our winter walking holiday.

We've built in plenty of flexibility around our activities to allow for my energy levels. I'm not sure how much walking I'll be able manage nor whether my wound will be watertight for swimming, but I'm feeling optimistic!

I'm buzzing with energy as we head up the M6 and turn on to the A69 towards Hadrian's wall. I've already planned our first coffee stop at House of Meg (I've checked it's open, thank you Google Maps) in Gilsland. It's busy when we arrive - cyclists clad in colourful Lycra have filled all but one of the picnic tables on the green outside.

After refuelling, we head cross country to Housesteads Roman Fort for some history and a stroll along Hadrian's wall. I can't believe we've never been here before. I love ruins! It's a self-guided tour (we had to book ahead due to Covid) and is free for National Trust members. Housesteads boasts what I think must be the most well-preserved Roman latrine in the country. The Romans were well ahead of the Britons when it came to sanitation. Maybe they could teach us a thing or two today? As I WhatsApp my photo, my sister remarks on the lovely view from the loo! Erm, I think it had walls in those days...

What a fascinating place. And the weather is stunning, too. I've had my eye on the Ordnance Survey map and wonder whether I'll manage the walk, which is screaming 'come hither'. We ask at the visitors' centre and they confirm that it's an easy five kilometres or so along the most attractive stretch of the wall.

We walk the ten-kilometre round trip and concur that this is the most beautiful part of Hadrian's wall - from Housesteads to Steel Rigg and back. Wow, stunning! Ah, my legs are a bit tired now. After a short drive I collapse onto the bed at the very well-appointed Bowes Hotel in Bardon Mill. What a great place! Newly refurbished and very friendly. I recommend the pulled pork burger.

Sunday 9 August, 2020

Where shall we go today? I've done my research and I suggest to Steve that we can't go to Northumberland without visiting Holy Island. It's less than two hours' drive away and we're up early. We enjoy breakfast at our hotel and Steve announces the poached eggs are the best he's ever tasted. On our way out, we get chatting to our hostess who is from Thailand and the one responsible for our delicious breakfast. She's been busy renovating during lockdown and we congratulate her on her good taste and culinary skills.

I'm so chuffed by my progress on yesterday's walk that we decide to continue on foot to Holy Island (Lindisfarne), which lies across a causeway. We park the car then set off over the sands with a spring in our step, having consulted the tide timetable to make sure we won't be cut off. About two hours later we are still crossing the sandy wastes and Steve remarks that he hadn't quite appreciated how far it was. Never mind, once we arrive at the only town on the island, we love it. It's a good thing we walked too because the car park is eye-wateringly expensive, and heaving. We can't go in the priory as it's pre-bookings only, but we have a good view of the impressive ruins.

I've heard that the walk to the north coast is worthwhile, so I convince Steve to extend our exploration just a bit further. There are far fewer tourists here and we discover sand dunes, seals and a very inviting beach. As we head down the dunes to the beach, my body starts to yearn for the water and my mind spouts tendrils that delicately nudge at possibility. I've been dying to swim for a while but have desisted due to worry about my wound being slow to heal. I turn to Steve. He's read my mind. Is my wound sufficiently watertight? Yes, I'm sure it is and anyway, salt water will do it good! I'm grinning all over my face. It is such ecstasy to be in the water, and in such a special place.

Is there a bus to take us back over the causeway to save the six-kilometre return walk? Er, it's Sunday so buses aren't running. Oops! We've been keeping an eye on the time to make sure we're not wading back. We've heard stories about locals who know exactly how to time it in their four-by-fours, followed by tourists who are not so skilled at navigating an underwater causeway and end up floating out to sea! Some people try to emulate King Canute. Not us! Nothing else for it but to head back on foot. A few cheeky attempts at hitchhiking come to nothing (we tend to find tourists are not up for it in the same way mountaineers are) and we plod on across the sands while a steady stream of cars passes by. We almost manage to walk the whole way back on the sand but end up having to retrace our steps when the water channel, which looked so easy to jump, becomes that little bit too wide and deep, and Steve doesn't want to ruin his new boots in the salt water. By the time we reach the car, my Fitbit tells me we have walked over twenty kilometres.

Seahouses is the perfect base for the next two nights. We enjoy some well-deserved fish and chips sitting on the harbour wall in the evening sunshine. On the walk back to our hotel, we pass a co-op - a godsend! I'm starting to crave fruit after indulging in too many cooked breakfasts. We've managed to find the most inexpensive hotel in Seahouses, which is a little walk from the centre, but not an unpleasant one. The staff are very friendly, the room is comfortable (with complementary biscuits, which never go amiss) and there's even a beautiful beer garden.

Monday 10 August, 2020
The sun is blazing in a blue sky this morning.
'How about bussing it to Bamburgh and walking back along the sands?' I suggest to Steve.
'Excellent idea!' he agrees.
The bus leaves from just outside our hotel, and the grass in the beer garden is dry enough for me to do some yoga while we wait. To my amazement, I can do downward-facing dog without any pain in the muscles around my implant. Progress!
After exploring Bamburgh a little, we stop off in 'Doctors Lane' for a photo, grab a snack then rest on a bench by the perfectly manicured green outside the castle. It boasts a cricket pitch and croquet lawn, and some expert croquet players are pitting their skills against each other in a ferocious game, which provides us with great entertainment. From the beach, I take a photo of the castle silhouetted against a backlit sky and WhatsApp it to family, claiming to have built a very swanky sandcastle. They're not fooled.
Before we walk back to Seahouses along the sands, Steve sunbathes (I tell him not to let himself burn but he doesn't listen) while I run down to the sea for a dip. The water is fourteen-degrees Celsius and glorious! Two days in the sea in a row and I can't get enough. We cross miles of unspoilt white sands to return to Seahouses at a leisurely pace. What could be better?

Tuesday 11 August, 2020
Today we'll head to Edinburgh. It seems such a pity to leave the Northumberland beaches behind but when we booked the trip, we didn't know how much walking and outdoor stuff I would

manage so we went for two nights each in Edinburgh and Stirling. We're not due at our guesthouse until four and there's a storm coming from the north so to make the most of the Northumberland sunshine, we visit another gem, Low Newton-by-the-sea. The sands here are golden, in contrast to the white sands of Bamburgh, and it's just as beautiful. It's an old fishing village with a green quadrangle framed by whitewashed cottages. Nestled in one corner, the historic Ship Inn looks out over the beach and wild sea.

'Can we buy a cottage here?' Steve asks.

It's a couple of miles' walk along the beach (time for another swim), dunes and past the golf course to Dunstanburgh Castle, an impressive ruin whose edifice dominates the view. The castle is the main attraction between Low Newton and Craster, and all three can be visited on a circular walk which, according to *The Guardian* newspaper, is one of the UK's top walks. I can see why. We don't make it as far as Craster but halt at the castle for a picnic and some photos. We're not allowed in as you have to pre-book. Never mind, we need to head on to Edinburgh.

By the time we've retraced our steps to Low Newton, the green is seething with people and the queue for the pub is a mile long. Luckily there's someone leaning out of a hatch selling cups of tea, and a family have just vacated a table in the sunshine. Perfect!

After the empty country roads, it's a little stressful driving around Edinburgh trying to find our guesthouse. I overshoot it then have to dodge buses and local drivers to make a U-turn and find a parking space. What a place! It looks like a boudoir and Steve appreciates the picture of Marilyn Monroe on the wall.

It's a bit of a walk into the centre from Leith where we're staying, but we're not complaining. We find a pizzeria and gorge ourselves on the most enormous pizzas I've ever seen. Somehow, we manage to dodge a tropical storm that passes overhead while we eat. I also text my friend Emma, whom I've seen once in a blue moon since we were students at Somerville College in Oxford, to ask if she's free tomorrow. To my surprise she is and would love to meet up for coffee. Excellent!

Wednesday 12 August, 2020
We have only one full day in Edinburgh and oh my do we make the most of it. It's wall-to-wall sunshine after last night's storm and we set off on foot, having consulted Google Maps to plan a breakfast stop on our way into town. Emma has given us directions to Swedish cafe and bakery Soderberg on the Meadows. We cross Princes Street in the morning sunlight and head through the old town towards it. This is a part of Edinburgh we've not seen before and we love it. Over coffee, I regale Emma with my cancer horror story while Steve listens patiently to our girl chat. Emma's been offered a professorship in the US and plans to move in the new year. Wow!

We spend the day walking the length and breadth of the city, beginning with a trip to Arthur's Seat. Oh dear, urgent matters need to be settled before we hike up there. To my dismay, a lot of cafes, including the one that just served us a diuretic, have closed their loos and many public conveniences are also closed. Nightmare. Thankfully I discover a phone app that identifies public toilets and, feeling much relieved, find a scramble that takes us up to Arthur's Seat. The climb is well worth the panoramic view.

On the way down, I fancy an ice cream. We end up on the Royal Mile, which is heaving, and escape the crowds by diving into an ice-cream parlour. We've never heard of this brand but it's home-made, the portions are humongous and the taste is divine. They're reasonably priced, too. We have two scoops each because we reckon we've earned it after our hike.

Our next stop is Edinburgh Castle. Turns out it's closed but the sun is still shining so who wants to be inside a castle anyway? It's still afternoon as we pass some restaurants, but we realise we should have thought sooner about booking one for dinner. Everywhere is fully booked! Eventually we discover a Brazilian restaurant and manage to secure one of their outdoor tables for this evening. Not what we'd had in mind, but I'm always keen to extend my palate. What shall we do to fill the time? I'm flagging somewhat - I still struggle without an afternoon nap. We can't be bothered to go back to the guesthouse. How about a snooze on the grass in the park by Princes Street? Looks like it flooded last night and although the waters have receded, it's still rather waterlogged. We find a sunny spot that is not a bog and spread out our waterproofs as makeshift blankets. That's better. We have half an hour's shut eye, listening to the world go by.

On our way to dinner, we stop for an enormous gin. 'Before you go for your Brazilian,' quips Steve. We're a little early still so we pause to watch and gasp in awe at skateboarders in Bristo Square.

Twelve hours and 32,000 steps after we left the guesthouse we return, a little the worse for wear, but content in the knowledge that we didn't waste a single moment of our day. I did miss going for a swim though!

Thursday 13 August, 2020
Six weeks post-op
On to Stirling. It's a pleasant and leisurely drive but the weather has turned rather nippy. Not raining though. We find our hotel with no bother then we're off to explore. We're desperate for a coffee and choose the first coffee house we stumble upon, the Hemp Cafe. It's an unpretentious, down-to-earth place – an instant tick in my good books. The waitress asks whether we'd like CBD oil added to our lattes. Pardon? Yes, it's the new craze. It doesn't contain the psychoactive substance from cannabis (THC) but has proven health benefits, apparently. Well, we're on holiday, why not? I allow her to talk me into doubling the cost of our drinks with this anxiety-alleviating, tumour-busting, sleep-enhancing, pain-relieving elixir. On our way out, Steve announces that he feels no different after the most expensive coffee we've ever bought. He doesn't rate 'this hemp stuff'. I point out to him that he's been putting hemp cream on his face for the past ten

years at least. Does he not recognise the shape of the leaf pictured on the front?

Friday 14 August, 2020
We like Stirling. Steve is happy to find a guitar shop as well as a vinyl record shop, and I'm happy exploring the cemetery. I am a big fan of cemeteries. I love to imagine the people who were here before me by reading their names, when and how old they were when they died, and the nature of any inscriptions about them. We also discover more good coffee houses and a fabulous cafe which serves the best borscht I've tasted outside of Moscow (complete with a generous dollop of smetana). I've been looking forward to our visit to Stirling Castle for ages. My favourite queen was crowned there when she was just nine months old. Poor baby, she didn't know what she had coming to her! It's a bit of a shame that the main indoor areas are closed due to Covid, but the castle is well worth a visit.

From the castle we can see the Wallace monument, which is calling me to climb up to it. We still have the whole afternoon, so I suggest we walk there. I'm convinced the map shows that we can cut through the industrial estate but there's a high fence blocking our way so we are forced to go the long way round. It's a bit of a climb through the woods to reach the monument, which is closed but rather impressive nonetheless. We make it back down to a cafe in time for a cup of tea and are assailed by midges which emerge from nowhere to feast on our tender flesh.

Saturday 15 August, 2020
We are on our way home feeling exhausted but happy. What a shame our holiday has to end! During lockdown, Steve and I discovered the Outlander boxset and he's convinced the film studio is somewhere around here. Unfortunately it's closed but we discover one of the filming locations is enroute so we swing by Doune Castle (also of *Monty Python* and *Game of Thrones* fame). Ooh, what a fab place. Shame we can't climb over the ramparts

and explore. Wait - is there a river down there? I wonder if it's swimmable? Yes!

I wade into the Teith river for one last swim. As I allow its cool waters to wash over me, I feel that not only my holiday, but my six-month hike on the dark side, are complete.

Chapter 17

Has Cancer Changed You?

'Has cancer changed you?' Steve asks as I reach over to turn out the bedside light a night or two before returning to work.

'Why do you ask? Do you think I've changed?'

'I don't think so,' he says.

Maybe it's the imminence of my return to work that makes him feel the need to punctuate this paragraph in our life. It's a relief to hear that he doesn't think I've changed. At least, not for the worse! I'm still fundamentally me. But my response is yes, cancer has changed me. How could it not?

It is human nature to try to make sense of bad things when they happen to us. Resilience training aims to minimise the risk of PTSD by teaching soldiers to make sense of the traumatic events they experience. If we can write our experiences into our life's narrative and make a coherent story, we feel much more at home in our own skin. During my seemingly interminable wait for surgery, Merryn helped me to make some sense of what I was going through with our guided meditations. I often think of the meditation in which I encountered a tiny, delicate flower growing in a wood. It would have been easily trampled underfoot had it not been for its striking appearance, which made people step over or around it. That flower was me. Before I was forced to slow down by my cancer diagnosis, I would not have noticed the flower as I powered past on my hike. I'd probably have stepped on it.

I've always been hard on myself. I would never berate my patients if they didn't live up to their own standards or if they didn't excel all the time in everything they did. I don't think this tendency will ever leave me entirely but being forced to take time off work and face some of my demons has allowed me to forgive myself for not being perfect. I am now practicing being kind to myself when I feel like I don't measure up, and I am beginning to take myself less seriously. We all make mistakes and none of us are indispensable. Neither of these are bad things. If we can remember them then we no longer need to cling for dear life to our self-esteem.

I still don't think there is a reason why I got breast cancer. Nor do I believe there is a reason why I am infertile when I so desperately want a family. Sometimes shit happens. It's how you deal with the shit that matters. I hate it when people say everything happens for a reason - so I wasn't meant to have children, is that it? No. I've done my fair share of railing against God, screaming at the top of my lungs, 'Why do you hate me?' God doesn't hate me, but I won't understand his reasons, at least not in this life.

Thomas Chisholm wrote:

> Great is thy faithfulness, oh God my father,
> There is no shadow of turning with thee;
> Thou changest not. Thy compassions they fail not...
> Morning by morning new mercies I see;
> All I have needed thy hand has provided...

And that's the funny thing. I have always somehow had the strength to cope with the shitstorms life has thrown at me. It may not feel like it at the time, but our experiences mould us into who we are and what we are becoming.

I like to think that this experience has helped me to be less overcome by setbacks. I have become slower and calmer and have less of a tendency to panic if I can't find the solution immediately. Long may this last!

Many things about me haven't changed. When I heard I would need major surgery, I was terrified that my body would be horribly disfigured and I would lose my athletic figure. My six pack isn't what it was, but I still cut it in Lycra and I even get whistled at from time to time! I see no reason why I shouldn't recover my peak level of fitness. I also retain my insatiable intellectual curiosity (I now know an awful lot about breast cancer) and my tendency to give my whole self to things with gay abandon. So thank you cancer, you have made me more myself, not less.

Oddly enough, having cancer has also challenged me to face the grief of my childlessness. Unlike many other women, my cancer did not cause my childlessness. Did my childlessness cause my cancer? I don't know, but stress and grief are part of the aetiology, I am sure. Before I knew that I was unable to have children, I couldn't even contemplate the idea. When you are going through IVF, you must believe it's going to work. Why would you do it otherwise?

When I did IVF, it was taboo - not something you talked about. While I was quite open about it, I received nothing like the same degree of understanding and concern that having cancer brought me. Somehow having cancer makes you a worthy person, deserving of special treatment, care and compassion. Friends, family, colleagues and even strangers were so kind to me when they heard I had cancer. I felt so validated, such a sense of belonging. When you have cancer, everyone asks how you are, and people cut you some slack when you're not firing on all four cylinders. It's OK to be feeling sad or apprehensive. Childlessness is not something you feel able to share without inviting judgement, pity or derision. That or just a complete inability to fathom why it's even an issue. Comments like 'Have some of mine!', 'At least you can travel!', 'You still have your health' or 'It must be nice to get so much sleep' sting. But the way you beat yourself up is far worse: 'If only I'd not been so picky about finding the right man until it was too late', 'It must be because I'm not fit to be a mother' or 'I can't have wanted it enough or tried hard enough'. I never thought that way about my cancer. It was just bloody bad luck and I could deal with it. I didn't need to soul search to figure out why I had cancer or what I had done to cause it.

I had no idea that what I was feeling was grief until I joined Gateway Women, a community of childless women. We call it disenfranchised grief: nobody died, there is nothing tangible to hold onto and we have no happy memories to anchor us. Just a great big gaping hole left by what never was, is not and never will be. At first, I thought I wouldn't survive. The emotional pain was indescribable - all my empty tomorrows stretching in front of me for ever and ever. But I did survive, because I had to. With the help of Gateway Women, I have learned to grow around my grief, and celebrate what I have rather than dwelling on what I don't have. At the same time, I still honour my grief and that visceral longing to touch my children, which will always be with me.

It sounds weird but unlike my childlessness, I don't really hold the fact that I had cancer against God. It was more a case of, 'Oh, thanks Lord, you have a really sick sense of humour – help me to get through this!' Childlessness has been a completely different kettle of fish and try as I might, I couldn't forgive Him for it. With cancer there is resolution. Even when I was in COVID-19 limbo with no idea when I would have my mastectomy, I knew it would happen sooner or later. With childlessness there is no resolution. There is no cure. But you can still *live*. When I was trying to disentangle my grief of childlessness from my anger about having cancer, Merryn showed me there are aspects of my life that would not have been possible if I had children. It's not the path I would have chosen but it is the path I am on and it is a good one.

I find it almost impossible not to play the comparison game. I consider my experience of cancer to have been a walk in the park compared to that of other cancer patients. I didn't have to endure chemo or radiotherapy, nor did I suffer the indignity caused by many other types of cancer. As my mother-in-law said, you can do without a breast! I might have thought differently had I been throwing up from chemo, or had to get used to a colostomy bag, or been forced to endure paroxysms of excruciating pain, but I can only speak from my own experience. Of course, secondary cancer is another thing entirely. I can't even imagine how I would come to terms with that. I have huge admiration for those who remain positive against all odds.

Of course, some big positives to come out of my cancer experience have been remembering my love of painting and the joy it brings me, taking up yoga and meditation, and I would never have become a blogger had it not been for breast cancer. Above all, it has led me to wild swimming and mountain pursuits which make my heart sing and my skin zing.

I started swimming in the river Kent in April, 2020 having never thought about doing so before. It was not my intention to go for a swim but as I walked along the bank, the water beckoned and before I knew it, I was an addict. There are definite perks to working from home two days per week: I now plan my timetable to include an hour's lunch break for a 'jog-swim', which has become my staple. I cannot overstate how much it helps my mental health. The six-week break from swimming that I was forced to take after surgery was torture. That said, I knew that I would be able to get back in the water sooner or later. My first dip in the North Sea off Holy Island was out of this world.

After returning from our holiday, I immediately resumed my Monday/Tuesday jog-swims to the river Kent, although the jog part was more walk to start with. I was ultra-cautious about resuming running and waited almost eight weeks after my surgery before donning my running shoes and jogging - very slowly - over the Helm. I was horrified to find that my VO2max (the maximum rate of oxygen your body is able to use during exercise) had gone down from 43 to 36, and it's been a struggle to get it back up. I have longstanding aches and pains in my hips (too much long-distance running in my twenties) so I can't run further than ten kilometres, and usually limit it to about six or seven, including some hills to push my heart rate right up.

The week before I returned to work, I discovered Gurnal Dubs, a mountain tarn above Staveley in the South Lakes. More? The Artisan Bakery in Mill Yard sells hot chocolate and ginger Sticky Nicky cake (a northern England speciality) to die for. It is just the thing when you arrive from the run covered in mud and soaking wet! The leg-punishing run up to the tarn is about 300 metres of height gain, followed by a 500-metre-ish swim and a happy, galumphing dash back down. I neither run nor swim elegantly but who cares? It feels so good to be alive!

I love the gasping, heart-racing shock of first contact with cold water. You know that moment when you can't help shrieking with both cold and delight. I take a pair of goggles for swims in the river, but when I'm on a mountain walk, I leave them behind as I prefer it to be an experience rather than a race, and if I swim breaststroke, I can keep my head above the water.

The benefits of cold-water swimming are well known but for me, it puts me on a high and leaves me gasping for more. I have joined the outdoor swimming society on Facebook for inspiration and tips on cold-water swimming. I was very touched to receive a wealth of good wishes when I posted a picture of my first post-cancer surgery swim. Wild swimming is such a tonic for the body and soul, and I will always be grateful that I discovered it on my cancer journey.

Afterword

They say six to eight weeks off work is the norm for a mastectomy with immediate implant reconstruction. I'm considered 'young and fit' in the breast cancer world so I expected to return sooner, but everyone warned me not to underestimate the psychological toll of breast cancer during the Covid pandemic. I took two months and I'm glad I heeded the advice because resuming work left me permanently exhausted.

My first few days back at work, though daunting, were a pleasure. The team were so delighted to see me that I felt wanted and needed. I also knew that it was time for me to move on from being a 'sick person' to being a 'recovered person'. But oh my, I wasn't ready for how tired I was going to feel. My 'phased return' went out the window because we were a doctor down and I had to take up the slack. Add to that the 'Covid contingency plan' decisions, which were made at my medical school during my absence, and I found myself playing catch up, big time. A year after the events in this book began, I am still tired and I head to bed at nine every night because I can't stay awake.

So how has the erstwhile patient resumed the role of doctor? My confidence is not what it was for I am no longer untouchable by death and decrepitude. I am not the only doctor to experience this: a GP colleague who had cancer a few years ago recently asked me how I was navigating my new identity as a doctor-patient. The trauma of being a cancer patient will affect both who I am and how I practice. I haven't thought about that explicitly before, but I'm starting to notice it. When a patient mentions to me that her experience of having breast cancer was a breeze compared to the depression she is now suffering, I'm tempted to compare notes. That wouldn't be professional though, would it? If my patients ask me how I am, I tell them; if not, I don't mention it. I also tend to play it down: 'Oh yes, I'm cancer-free now. I've been given the all-clear so I'm back to normal.' Am I? Will I ever be?

Survivor's guilt still plagues me at times, but mostly I'm just glad that I survived and that it wasn't worse. I'm also acutely aware of how lucky I was to have my surgery when I did. I wonder whether, had I not been a doctor, I'd have had the gumption to request a second opinion and to seek a unit that was ahead of the game with its resumption of surgery.

I also feel the need to justify my decision to stop taking tamoxifen. If I wasn't a doctor, I don't think I'd have questioned my right to stop taking it. And nowadays I'm much more inclined to listen to a patient when they tell me they are experiencing side effects from their medication. If they understand the risks of not taking the medication, then it's up to them whether they take it or not.

So, was I right to have stopped taking tamoxifen? On the one hand I feel guilty that I might be costing the NHS more money in the future if I do end up with another breast cancer. Taking tamoxifen for five years would reduce my risk by thirty to fifty percent. However, as my risk is just four percent, that means it would only reduce to two or three percent and the tamoxifen made me feel horrible. I felt abnormal, as if I couldn't access my joyful emotions so I felt glum all the time. I'm not willing to live like that to reduce my risk of another breast cancer by two percent. Am I being selfish? Maybe, then again, I'm the one who has to live my life so I must live it on my own terms.

Tamoxifen also ruined my sex life. Both Steve and I were worried about how it would be after my surgery but it was a big weight off both our minds when nothing changed for the worse in the bedroom. At least not at first. I started to notice something was wrong with me after I'd been on tamoxifen for just over two weeks. On the first day of our holiday in Northumberland, Steve and I were enjoying a leisurely 'cuddle' in our rather lovely room in the Bowes Hotel. I still felt desire, but I just couldn't seem to 'get there'. Something felt different with my physiology.

I am fortunate that cancer has not diminished my sex drive one bit, other than to deprive me of one erogenous zone (left nipple). At least I still have one left. I am very lucky that my new fake boob looks symmetrical and very similar to my real one, and Steve still fancies me. He also keeps forgetting that the new boob has no sensation. We have always enjoyed a very satisfying sex life and I have every intention of that continuing. Even through the heartbreak of learning of my infertility, we managed to retain our intimacy. One perk of having no little ones around is the opportunity to have sex whenever you like. Tamoxifen put the kibosh on my ability to enjoy one of the pleasures of my childless life.

Taking tamoxifen also caused my periods to stop so when I came off it, they started again with a vengeance. Not only that but throughout November, I was bleeding nearly every day. It wasn't like a normal period, it was light but persistent. I suspected it was my hormones correcting themselves, as well as the perimenopause reasserting itself. However, I couldn't ignore abnormal bleeding so I contacted the GP who sent me for an urgent hysteroscopy. It's highly unlikely that I had endometrial cancer but given that tamoxifen is known to cause it, we decided to err on the side of caution. After all, it was highly unlikely that I had breast cancer until I had breast cancer.

As soon as I knew I was going for more cancer investigations, I was thrown right back into the trauma of my cancer experience. I had reawakened the nightmare of waiting for appointments and test results. I felt anxious and found it hard to concentrate. My clinics were very busy during the two-week wait for an appointment date, and I was constantly on tenterhooks over whether I was going to need to cancel a clinic at short notice. I kept having flashbacks to that day in breast clinic in February 2020, when I had to cancel my afternoon clinic while grappling with the idea that I might have breast cancer. I didn't know whether I could book meetings with medical students or commit to teaching sessions either. How could I plan when I didn't know when the procedure was going to be or if I'd need a day off work to recover? Plus, it was almost Christmas. Steve was anxious for me, and we both felt frustrated and on edge.

Nearly a week after the referral, I had ants in my pants because my appointment still hadn't come through. I couldn't sit still or concentrate. I contacted a gynaecologist friend and asked if she could do me a very big favour and chase it up. What would I do without nepotism? It wasn't necessary in the end because that evening I was offered an appointment for two days later. I decided to take it even though it meant curtailing my Thursday clinic.

As sod's law would have it, that clinic was the worst I have ever had. I was on edge because I'd heard that having a hysteroscopy was far from pleasant, but what bothered me more was the fear that my clinic would run over and make me late or even miss my appointment. I also felt guilty that I was rushing and not entirely focused on my patients. To make matters worse, I had two medical students to supervise and felt bad I was abandoning them halfway through the afternoon. I ended up dashing out the door, leaving a pile of unfinished paperwork and feeling like I'd had a day from hell.

I did make it to my appointment in time (huge thank you to Steve for driving me there!) though I can safely say that I am in no hurry whatsoever to repeat a day such as that one. It took me over a week to recover from the shock of another cancer scare, and I was a wreck for a while even though my uterus looked normal. It brought home to me just how, once you've been a cancer patient, you are always living in its shadow.

I'm in the business of diagnosing dementia. Since my seemingly interminable wait and the uncertainty surrounding my breast cancer diagnosis (which wasn't finalised until after surgery), I have a whole lot more empathy for my patients who are waiting to hear their diagnosis. Waiting is torture. That said, sometimes diagnoses are complicated to make and resources are scarce. My patients' diagnoses are normally delayed by a month while we wait for their brain scan. This delay does not put them in any danger because dementia is incredibly slow to develop, but it does mean a diagnosis we could make within two weeks takes about six. How do we balance the need for diagnostic accuracy against expedience?

In the case of my breast cancer, the initial plan was the COVID-19 pathway for DCIS - 'review in three months'. As a doctor, I was in the privileged position of being able to source a second opinion with relative ease but even then, the MRI that suggested invasive disease didn't happen until three months after my symptoms started. In the end the wait did not affect my prognosis, as my invasive ductal carcinoma was Grade 1 with no lymph node spread. But isn't that just luck? How do I learn from my own experience without over-investigating all my patients and feeling terrible if they have to wait any longer than absolutely necessary for their diagnosis?

I'm now up to running twice a week or so, wild swimming as often as I can, and I spend a day each weekend hiking up mountains, but I still don't feel anywhere near as fit as I did before my surgery. My implant seems fine when I run as long as I wear a mega-supportive bra, but my pectoral muscles on that side are a little sore to the touch. The swelling I originally had around the implant has subsided and it now looks very pert and much less droopy than my normal breast (even with zero ptosis). I've got the tiniest bit of cording but nothing that bears mention and it's not restricting me. I may have some capsular contraction - the pictures I found online all look horrendous and mine looks nothing like those, but it does feel very tight. There is no sign of any sensation returning to my salvaged skin yet, but my armpit is gaining a little more feeling.

I'm still convinced that the best thing in the whole wide world is wild swimming. I've invested in a neoprene hat for the winter. No wetsuit! Whenever I see a body of water, I can't resist stripping down to my underwear (or birthday suit if there's no one around) and plunging in. Bring it on!

APPENDICES

Appendix A
Suspension of Elective Surgery Due to COVID-19

Throughout the spring lockdown of 2020, the UK government was adamant that the NHS was open for business as usual, and it became their mantra at the daily coronavirus briefing. However, the reality on the ground was that, at the start of lockdown, large numbers of NHS staff were off sick or self-isolating because they were unable to get tested (myself included), and non-COVID-19 services ground to a halt. Our own service in older adult community mental health was a case in point. On 13 March, we were issued a mandate to suspend memory clinic assessments and all 'non-urgent' appointments until further notice. The NHS became a COVID-19-only service.

Worldwide, breast cancer surgery came to standstill. On 15 March in the UK, the Association of Breast Surgery issued the following recommendations to breast surgeons for the COVID-19 pandemic:

'These are extremely difficult times for everyone in the health service. Although our aim would be to run a normal breast service, it is unlikely that we are going to be able to do this in the coming weeks. We suggest that you develop a plan now so that this can be implemented as the pandemic worsens. With the potential shortage of medical staff and theatres, we are all going to have to adapt and prioritise the order in which breast cancer patients receive surgical treatment.'

On Thursday 26 March, 2020 the NHS England and The Federation of Surgical Specialty Associations (a collaborating body bringing together multiple surgical specialities in the UK) published detailed guidelines on prioritisation of patients for surgery during the COVID-19 pandemic. All 'elective' surgery (which includes all cancer surgery) was suspended. Prioritisation levels were introduced:

Priority 1a Emergency - operation needed within 24 hours.
Priority 1b Urgent - operation needed within 72 hours.
Priority 2 Surgery that can be deferred for up to 4 weeks.
Priority 3 Surgery that can be deferred for up to 3 months.
Priority 4 Surgery that can be deferred for > 3 months.

There was a blanket ban on breast reconstructions. Patients who needed an urgent mastectomy, where it was deemed 'unsafe to wait', had their mastectomy within a fairly normal timeframe (priority level 2), but all reconstructions were cancelled. Breast reconstructions fell under priority level 4. You can 'safely' wait forever for a breast reconstruction. The trouble is, this rule created an even greater backlog in breast reconstructions than before COVID-19. The preferred method of reconstruction, be it implant or autologous tissue, is to do it immediately, at the same time as the mastectomy, unless radiation therapy is required. Delayed reconstruction has worse aesthetic and surgical outcomes. Breast Cancer Now estimates that the March suspension of NHS breast reconstructions services resulted in 1000 women missing out on immediate reconstruction and around 500 on delayed reconstruction.

On 3 April, Hospital A categorised me as level 4: although I was pre-menopausal, low-grade DCIS fell under 'safe to wait at least three months'. At the time it didn't occur to them that there might be something invasive lurking amid all those abnormal calcifications in my breast.

You might ask why cancer surgery is deemed 'elective'. It doesn't feel very elective if you've been diagnosed with cancer and are waiting for a mastectomy. Dr Julie Sprunt put it very eloquently in this podcast on 3 April
(https://www.breastcancer.org/community/podcasts/breast-surgery-covid19-20200406):

'When we think of an elective surgery, we say that's a surgery that is not going to immediately threaten somebody's life or... limb, and all surgeries outside of that are considered to be elective... It's not that anybody is suggesting that breast cancer surgery is something that somebody can elect to have or not, but it means that there is a large subset of women with breast cancer in whom we can safely use a non-operative treatment strategy so that their surgery does become less urgent. We... can safely delay many women's breast cancer operations. Not because they're elective, but because that is what we are being asked to do when we look at the resources that we currently have in this country as we approach and are going through a national disaster.'

As events unfolded, surgeons were busy working behind the scenes to do what they could to minimise the damage caused by Covid to cancer services and other 'elective' surgeries. In a bizarre sort of way, I was heartened to hear the situation was the same all over the world. In the rest of Europe and in the USA, all elective surgery was postponed. Ironically, on 3 April, the day I received my diagnosis and was told I needed a mastectomy, Dr Elisabeth Potter, an oncoplastic/breast surgeon from Texas, said this to her patients in a podcast (https://www.breastcancer.org/podcast/breast-surgery-covid-19):

> 'I recognise that this is a frightening time. I don't want anyone who is going through breast cancer wondering, Am I being left behind? Does anyone remember me? I see you and I'm thinking about you and I am planning for your surgery. We just aren't operating right now.'

I found it very reassuring just to hear her say that. The news I had just been given, that I would have to wait at least three months for surgery, certainly made me feel left behind and forgotten.

By the end of April, surgeons were starting to get itchy feet. On 27 April, the Association of Breast Surgery issued another statement:

'Although in many parts of the UK it would appear that we have now reached the peak of COVID-19, we still face the uncertainty as to the future course of the pandemic. It appears that COVID-19 will be with us for many months, and attention locally and nationally is turning to how we deliver cancer services safely in this 'new normal'. Breast units in the UK have been extraordinarily proactive in continuing appropriate care for the benefit of our patients…

'Surgery
As more theatre space becomes available, we would recommend prioritising patients as follows:
- ER- patients (cancers that are not sensitive to oestrogen)
- HER2+ patients {cancers that have high levels of human epidermal growth factor, sensitive to Herceptin}
- Pre-menopausal patients & high-risk ER+ post-menopausal patients, ie. Grade 3 or node-positive patients (cancers that are sensitive to oestrogen and more aggressive cancer grades)
- Large areas of high-grade DCIS
- Post-menopausal ER+ lower-risk patients
- Remaining DCIS patients

'Benign breast surgery, prophylactic surgery and delayed reconstruction should still be on hold.

'Surgeons should think very carefully before embarking on immediate breast reconstruction, in particular implant reconstruction with its relatively higher levels of post operative infection and readmission rates. At present immediate breast reconstruction should still not be offered to the majority of patients.'

In theory, from this point onwards, the blanket ban on reconstructions was lifted. However, it is clear that great caution was advised before even considering immediate reconstruction, especially with implants. Having worked in the NHS for twenty years, I am familiar with this giant machine that moves very slowly. The positive correlate of the last statement, 'immediate breast reconstruction should be offered to a suitable minority of patients' was shelved in the 'too hard' pigeonhole. On 25 May, the Association of Breast Surgery published 'Moving Forward - Recommendations From the Association of Breast Surgery on Delivery of Breast Services During the COVID-19 Pandemic'. The prospects for breast reconstruction began to look a little more hopeful:

'Breast Reconstruction: All units performing immediate breast reconstruction (both implant and free-flap reconstruction) should now be working on an operations manual, which involves all stakeholders in their Trust. This should ensure that breast reconstruction can be delivered safely in their individual unit. This manual should include pathways for pre, intra and post-operative care, and should include robust pathways for patients who develop complications. We continue to advise a cautious approach in view of the significant risk of post-operative re-admission, return to theatre and infection. Once immediate breast reconstruction re-starts there will be an inevitable limitation in the number of reconstructions that can be performed because of ongoing precautions, including increased anaesthetic and recovery time and PPE requirements.'

On 27 May, Hospital B held a meeting to plan the resumption of reconstructive surgery. My surgeon phoned me immediately afterwards to let me know that he wanted to do my surgery at the end of June. I later found out via the Cancer Chat forum that immediate implant reconstructions had restarted in some parts of the country. As ever, there was great heterogeneity between NHS Trusts. All were working to an operation's manual, with patient criteria and pre-, intra-, and post-operative processes. And it goes without saying that surgery had to be carried out in Covid-free zones, with appropriate PPE (personal protective equipment) and stringent infection control measures.

Patient criteria

Pre-menopausal patients with breast cancer requiring unilateral mastectomy with immediate unilateral reconstruction (that's me). BMI less than 32 (my BMI is 21ASA1/2 - American Society of Anaesthesiologists physical rating scale: 1 means physically healthy). All patients discussed in MDT which includes an anaesthetist (they were discussing me every week!).

Pre-op

Minimise face-to-face contact through use of remote consultation where possible. Single clinic visit for pre-op-planning and pre-op assessment.
Self-isolation for 14 days. RT-PCR swab test 48-72 hours pre-op, only proceed if negative. Include Covid risks in consent form.

Quite simple really! Everything was poised to swing into action as soon as the Trust gave the go-ahead to resume breast reconstructions.

On 12 June, the British Association of Plastic, Reconstructive and Aesthetic surgeons (BAPRAS) held a webinar about resuming breast reconstructions, specifically autologous tissue reconstructions. I was unaware this webinar was taking place at the time, but later discovered it in my extensive research to find out what was happening behind the scenes during my seemingly interminable wait for surgery.

Adam Gilmour, a plastic surgeon from Glasgow, made the case for the resumption of free-flap reconstruction (not suitable for me because I didn't have enough fat to make a flap, plus the recovery time is longer). The passion with which he spoke about not only free-flap reconstruction but also implants and oncoplastic procedures was music to my ears. He emphasised the importance of working together to make things happen and to be the best advocates for our patients. He made the point that there was significant heterogeneity across the county and that even before Covid, depending on where they lived, patients were not always able to access the right treatment for them. Every woman is different and each needs to have the opportunity to choose the best option for her. He challenged the widely bandied assumption that 'no one needs a breast reconstruction' and the assertion 'they can always have a delayed reconstruction'.

Even before Covid, some areas of the country had long waiting lists for delayed reconstruction. I had always been very clear that I did not want to have a delayed reconstruction because the aesthetic outcomes are far less favourable. Gilmour spelled it out in his talk. He pointed out that in orthopaedic surgery, procedures in which 'delay would prejudice outcome' were in priority level 2. Why are breast reconstructions in level 4? He and I would both argue that delay prejudices outcome. If you have a plain mastectomy and delayed reconstruction, you lose your skin, necessitating tissue expanders and several more surgeries to achieve the aesthetic result of an immediate implant. You remain a cancer patient for much longer, must take more time off work, face more uncertainty and potentially years of delay. Not to mention the psychological consequences of being flat on one side, and its impact on your sex life and body image. It's a no brainer.

References:

Association of Breast Surgeons (2020) *Moving forward - recommendations from the Association of Breast Surgery on delivery of breast services during the Covid-19 pandemic.* Available at: https://associationofbreastsurgery.org.uk/media/296474/may-abs-statement-final-250520.pdf.

Association of Breast Surgery (2020a) *Association of Breast Surgery statement, 27th April 2020.* Available at: https://associationofbreastsurgery.org.uk/media/252026/abs-statement-270420.pdf.

Association of Breast Surgery (2020b) *Statement from the association of breast surgery 15th March 2020: confidential advice for health professionals.* Available at: https://associationofbreastsurgery.org.uk/media/252009/abs-statement-150320-v2.pdf.

British Association of Plastic, Reconstructive and Aesthetic surgeons (2020) BAPRAS COVID-19 webinar: Free Flap Breast Reconstruction

Federation of Surgical Specialty Associations (2020). Clinical guide to surgical prioritisation during the Coronavirus pandemic. https://fssa.org.uk/_userfiles/pages/files/covid19/prioritisation_master_301020.pdf

Jallali, N., Hunter, J. E., Henry, F. P., Wood, S. H., Hogben, K., Almufti, R., Hadjiminas, D., Dunne, J., Thiruchelvam, P. T. R. and Leff, D. R. (2020) 'The feasibility and safety of immediate breast reconstruction in the COVID-19 era', *Journal of plastic, reconstructive & aesthetic surgery : JPRAS,* 73(11), pp. 1917-1923.

Sprunt, J. and Potter, E. 2020. Breast Surgery and Reconstruction During COVID-19. breastcancer.org.

208

Appendix B
Impact of COVID-19 on Cancer Services in the UK

At the time of writing, the impact of COVID-19 on cancer services in the UK is only just becoming apparent. The effects will continue to be felt for many years to come. Patients will be diagnosed with cancer at a later stage due to the interruption of screening programmes.

In April 2020, 79,573 patients saw a specialist after an urgent GP referral for suspected cancer, compared to 199,644 in April 2019 - a fall of sixty percent. In June 2020, eighty-seven percent of patients diagnosed with cancer had been waiting more than two months for treatment and by July, only 319 patients whose cancer was identified by screening started treatment, compared to 1,890 the previous year, according to the Health Foundation. I cannot believe that there were eighty-three percent fewer cases of cancer in July 2020 than in July 2019.

My interpretation of these figures is that there are thousands of people with undiagnosed cancer in the UK because of the pandemic. And that's only the number that wasn't picked up by screening. Add to that the people who have delayed approaching a doctor about their lump or their bleeding nipple, or whatever other symptoms may herald cancer.

The British Medical Association (BMA) estimates that during March, April and May 2020, there were:

- Between 274,000 and 286,000 fewer urgent cancer referrals.
- Between 20,800 and 25,900 fewer patients starting first cancer treatment following decision to treat.
- Between 12,000 and 15,000 fewer patients starting first cancer treatment following urgent GP referral.

In April 2020, urgent GP cancer referrals were only forty-two percent of the previous year's average. In May 2020, first cancer treatments following decision to treat were sixty-five percent of the average for the previous two years.

Approximately 50,000 women are diagnosed with breast cancer per year in the UK. Normally the overall survival rate is greater than eighty-five percent. In the six months from January to June 2020, there was a forty percent reduction in non-urgent and a twenty-three percent reduction in urgent referrals for suspected breast cancer. The number of patients receiving their first treatment for breast cancer was sixteen percent lower than the previous year, although more than nine ty-five percent were treated within thirty-one days of decision to treat (due to the increased use of hormonal therapy as a stopgap because surgery was unavailable). There were 4,000 fewer cases of breast cancer diagnosed in the first six months of 2020 compared to the previous year.

When I think about my own care, I wonder where the clock started ticking on the time from decision to treat to treatment. Did seeking a second opinion reset the clock? Hospital A told me I needed surgery on April 3, but I could afford to wait at least three months. The result of my final investigation and a more definitive diagnosis (indicating that I could not afford to wait) did not come until May 20 via Hospital B. In effect, although my symptoms started in February, the time between decision to treat and surgery was only five weeks.

Data from Public Health England, revealed by Cancer Research UK, shows there were 7,700 fewer breast cancer surgeries carried out in England between April and August 2020 than the same period in 2019 (a thirty-nine percent reduction). Several complicated studies have recently modelled the impact of treatment delay on cancer mortality. Hanna and colleagues used twenty years of published studies to conclude that each four-week delay from diagnosis to surgery for all breast cancers increased the chance of death by eight percent. Wow.

Interestingly, Mateo and colleagues investigated the reasons for delays in surgery (pre COVID-19) and found the strongest predictor of longer time to surgery was mastectomy with reconstruction. Each month's delay increased mortality by about ten percent, regardless of breast cancer type. They also emphasised how delay in referral for suspected cancer of all types can have a big impact on survival. Even though the reduction in survival for low-grade cancers is small, the sheer number of these common cancers translates into many life years lost. They demonstrated that life years lost from delayed cancer treatment far outweighed those gained from hospital care for community-acquired COVID-19 patients. They urged that referral for patients under seventy years old should not be delayed, as a cancer caught at an earlier stage could mean the difference between curative surgery and lifelong treatment of secondary cancer.

How many patients will end up with secondary cancer due to the Covid pandemic? I shudder to think. One recent example is pop star Sarah Harding of Girls Aloud who, in the middle of a pandemic, didn't want to bother her doctor with her breast lump. By the time she did, the cancer had spread to her bones.

Bibliographic sources:

British Medical Association (2020) *The hidden impact of COVID-19 on patient care in the NHS in England*: British Medical Association. Available at: https://www.bma.org.uk/media/2841/the-hidden-impact-of-covid_web-pdf.pdf.

Courtney, A., et al. (2020) 'The B-MaP-C study: Breast cancer management pathways during the COVID-19 pandemic. Study protocol', *International journal of surgery protocols,*24, pp. 1-5.

The Health Foundation (2020) *Non-COVID-19 NHS care during the pandemic. Activity trends for key nHS services in England.* Available at: https://www.health.org.uk/news-and-comment/charts-and-infographics/non-covid-19-nhs-care-during-the-pandemic.

Gathani, T., Clayton, G., MacInnes, E. and Horgan, K. (2020) 'The COVID-19 pandemic and impact on breast cancer diagnoses: what happened in England in the first half of 2020', *British Journal of Cancer*.

Maringe, C. et al. (2020) 'The impact of the COVID-19 pandemic on cancer deaths due to delays in diagnosis in England, UK: a national, population-based, modelling study', *The Lancet Oncology,* 21(8), pp. 1023-1034.

Sud, A. et al. (2020a) 'Collateral damage: the impact on outcomes from cancer surgery of the COVID-19 pandemic', *Annals of Oncology,* 31(8), pp. 1065-1074.

Sud, A. et al (2020b) 'Effect of delays in the 2-week-wait cancer referral pathway during the COVID-19 pandemic on cancer survival in the UK: a modelling study', *The Lancet Oncology,* 21(8), pp. 1035-1044.

Appendix C
Tamoxifen

If you're premenopausal and have had surgery for an invasive, oestrogen receptor-positive (ER+) breast cancer, it is recommended that you take tamoxifen for five to ten years. There is robust evidence that tamoxifen improves your chance of survival: the NHS Predict tool tells me my fifteen-year survival improves from 96 percent to 96.3 percent if I take tamoxifen for five years, and it can reduce the risk of developing cancer in the other breast by 30 percent. I hesitated to start taking it as I'd heard all sorts of horror stories about side effects such as hot flushes, night sweats, vaginal dryness, menstrual irregularities, weight gain, blood clots and endometrial (womb) cancer. However, when you're already in perimenopause, it is difficult to tell whether any changes in menopause symptoms are tamoxifen-related or not. My breast surgeon friend urged me to at least try it to reduce the risk of cancer in the other breast. She said most people don't get side effects. I beg to differ. Tamoxifen rendered me anorgasmic.

I have a PhD in pharmacology, so if I need to take a medication, I like to research its mechanism of action to understand exactly what it's doing to my body. The pharmacodynamics (what the drug does to the body) and pharmacokinetics (what the body does to the drug) of tamoxifen are mind boggling to me. I'm sure not everyone shares my fascination for how drugs work but this is an interesting one. Here is my attempt to understand how tamoxifen works - buckle in, it's quite a ride!

Tamoxifen was initially developed in 1962 as a safe contraceptive, but funnily enough it ended up having exactly the opposite of the desired effect: it made women ovulate, rather than stop it. Unbeknown to its manufacturer ICI (now AstraZeneca), it was to become the first non-toxic targeted treatment for breast cancer, thanks in large part to collaboration between researchers and the enthusiasm of a young post-doc, VC Jordan, in examining its anti-tumour effects with some oh-so-elegant science.

Jordan discovered that tamoxifen was something known as a SERM (selective oestrogen-receptor modulator), which means that it blocks oestrogen receptors in some tissues (such as breast tumours) and stimulates them in others (such as the uterus and bones). One thing which I hadn't appreciated about oestrogen receptors is there are two types: ERα and ERβ. When oestrogen binds to either of these, what happens inside the cell depends on a variety of little helpers that send messages to turn the cell's genes on or off. In breast tumour cells, tamoxifen blocks the oestrogen receptors and this causes the cells to die (apoptosis – I like to imagine the cells going 'pop!') but in other tissues (such as the endometrium in the uterus), it can act like oestrogen itself.

The intricacies of the human body never cease to fascinate and amaze me. What my body does to a drug may be different to what another person's body does to the same drug. We all have different versions of our genes (polymorphisms) so the variety of a particular gene I have determines what happens to tamoxifen inside my body. Tamoxifen needs to be chomped on by the liver before it can carry out its business (it's the active metabolites that do the work – tamoxifen on its own seems inactive), and some people's livers seem to do this job better than others. In addition, my oestrogen receptors will not be the same as another woman's, so it's hard to predict whether the tamoxifen will be a wonder drug for me or whether it will just give me loads of side effects with few benefits. That said, on paper the benefits certainly have me convinced that it's worth a try.

My fascination doesn't stop there. Tamoxifen is also useful in preventing recurrence of oestrogen-negative cancers, although the way it does this is very confusing. I spent almost a whole day trying to get my head around it and I have to say that I am still rather bemused. Suffice to say that tamoxifen seems to have other actions as well as its action on the oestrogen receptor. It does something funny to mitochondria (the powerhouses that fuel our cells), which makes tumour cells more likely to pop and die. At the same time, it has strange effects on cholesterol metabolism which seems to protect against cancer. Paradoxically, while plenty of studies show that tamoxifen increases nasty oxygen-free radicals that damage cells (which is what you want to kill a tumour cell, but not what you want if the cell is healthy because it can cause it to malfunction), it also has antioxidant properties (and we all know that is a good thing). Tamoxifen also has direct effects on DNA, a mechanism by which it is thought to be good for treating cancers other than breast cancer.

With my psychopharmacologist's hat on, I also conducted a literature search to try to understand why I couldn't orgasm while on tamoxifen. Believe it or not, no one really understands the neurophysiology of female sexual arousal and orgasm (why does that not surprise me?). Now, as well as cancer and being infertile, my rather pesky recurrent mental illness means that I need to take antidepressants long term. Selective serotonin reuptake inhibitors (SSRIs) are notorious for causing sexual dysfunction and the one I take is no exception. However, until I started the tamoxifen the benefits of the SSRI outweighed the downsides: we could still, with a little battery-powered help, have a normal sex life. Yet while I was on tamoxifen, nothing - but nothing - worked! I have come to the conclusion there must be some interaction between serotonin and oestrogen that is necessary for the female orgasm pathway to function. Either tamoxifen or the SSRI alone may not be sufficient to kill it, but the combination is the nail in the coffin. The internet and the information sheet in the tamoxifen packet warn of common side effects, such as menopause-like symptoms. However, precious little is written about its sexual side effects, other than to say that the aromatase inhibitors are worse!

I tried topical oestrogen (not contraindicated in breast cancer) but was not surprised that it didn't make any difference as I believe the effects are in my central nervous system rather than 'down there'. I even considered reducing my SSRI dose or switching to another antidepressant with fewer sexual side effects. I decided against that because it carries the risk of a depressive relapse or winding up with different, but no less troublesome, side effects from the new antidepressant.

In the end, I managed to take tamoxifen for three months before I sacked it. Quite apart from putting the kibosh on my sex life, it made me feel glum all the time. Now, I know what it's like to feel depressed and it felt nothing like that. It just felt as though I was living in a grey world, and I was frustrated and irritable. Now, given that the PREDICT tool told me that tamoxifen would improve my fifteen-year survival by just 0.5 percent, I decided that feeling grim for five years was not a good trade off. I know that it reduces my risk of having cancer in the other breast, but I'm not willing to put up with feeling less than human for five years for the sake of something that may never happen. Does it sound awful to say I'd rather take the risk of having another mastectomy than take tamoxifen? I'd rather take my chances and hope we catch any incipient cancer with a yearly mammogram.

Further Reading

Goodsell DS. The molecular perspective: tamoxifen and the estrogen receptor. Oncologist. 2002;7(2):163-164.

Jordan VC. Tamoxifen: a most unlikely pioneering medicine. Nat Rev Drug Discov. 2003;2(3):205-213.

Shagufta, AHmmad I. Tamoxifen a pioneering drug: an update on the therapeutic potential of tamoxifen derivatives. Eur J Med Chem. 2018;143:515-531.

Yang G, Nowsheen S, Aziz K, Georgakilas AG. Toxicity and adverse effects of tamoxifen and other anti-estrogen drugs. Pharmacol Ther. 2013;139(3):392-404.

Appendix D
Not for the Squeamish

I can't apologise for being a doctor who has insatiable intellectual curiosity. When I was stuck at home, not allowed to do any of the things I love (mountain hiking, running, swimming), my mind turned to trying to understand my illness. I had some questions about breast surgery which none of the blogs, cancer information websites nor books I read could answer. So, I did some research of my own from the comfort of my sofa.

Why is my skin numb?
My least favourite aspect of my first year at medical school was the dissection lab. I defied my cadaver to teach me any anatomy whatsoever and to this day I still have great difficulty in visualising anatomical structures in 3D. Good thing I became a psychiatrist and not a surgeon! Luckily for me, some doctors who were very good at anatomy meticulously dissected the nerve supply of twelve breasts belonging to seven female cadavers (I warned you it wasn't for the squeamish). The paper they published explains why the skin over an implant is numb and illustrates it beautifully.

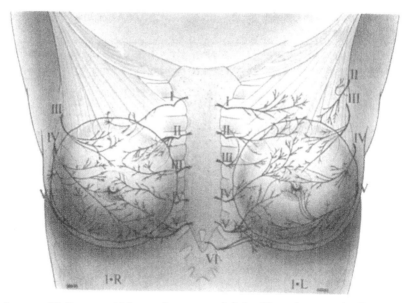

Jaspars JJ, Posma AN, van Immerseel AA, Gittenberger-de Groot AC. The cutaneous innervation of the female breast and nipple-areola complex: implications for surgery. Br J Plast Surg. 1997;50(4):249-259. doi:10.1016/s0007-1226(97)91155-3

The drawing shows that the breast skin is supplied by the lateral and anterior cutaneous branches of the nerves, which exit from between your vertebrae and run along your second to sixth ribs. If you trace a line down your chest from the middle of your armpit, that's where each upper intercostal nerve splits into anterior and lateral cutaneous branches which supply the breast (see picture below). The lateral branch finds its way out through some chest wall muscles then splits to supply the outer side of the breast and the armpit. The anterior branch runs deep under the muscles and pops up just next to the sternum, then splits to supply the skin over the sternum and the skin on the inner side of the breast. How elegant!

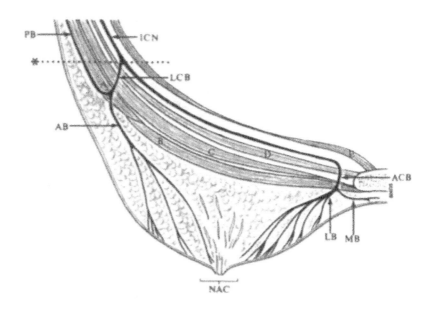

Horizontal cross section, also from Jaspars 1997

It's so fascinating! All the branches that supply the skin of the breast must be cut when a mastectomy is performed because they go right through the breast tissue before they end in the skin. Anyone who has a full mastectomy, especially with an implant reconstruction, will end up with severed nerves to the skin over the breast.

What's keeping my implant in?

Moving on from this exquisite artwork to my not-so-exquisite attempt to draw a cross section through my new boob (note that I've made it look larger than it really is!). The surgeon said I broke all records by having the smallest implant in history, at just 140ml).

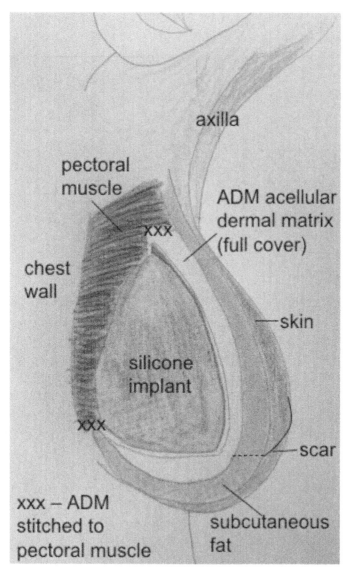

axilla

pectoral
muscle

xxx

ADM acellular
dermal matrix
(full cover)

chest
wall

skin

silicone
implant

xxx

scar

xxx – ADM
stitched to
pectoral muscle

subcutaneous
fat

Copied and personalised from Prepectoral Techniques in Reconstructive Breast Surgery, Ed. Gabriel et al., Lippincott Williams and Wilkins 2018

I drew this picture after I had a horrible nightmare in which my implant slid halfway down my tummy while I was jogging. It was probably my subconscious working overtime on the dire warnings from the breast care nurse to 'take it easy, otherwise you risk dislodging the implant!'

The implant is held in place - completely enclosed in front and behind - by a mesh called an acellular dermal matrix (ADM), made from the inner skin (dermis) of pigs. It's very clever stuff, especially for people like me who have rather thin skin without much fat under it. Over time it melds with your own skin to form a nice covering. It also makes the new boob much less likely to shrivel up like a desiccated orange (capsular contraction).

The surgeon laughed at me when I asked him how hard I'd have to work to dislodge the implant. 'The ADM is stitched quite firmly to the pectoral muscle above and below, you know!'

The trouble with having such thin skin is the ADM can ripple, and this can be visible through the skin. The surgeon did mention to me that if this becomes unsightly, I can have a procedure called lipomodelling. Adipose tissue is liposuctioned from one part of your body (usually belly fat) and centrifuged to isolate the fat cells, which are then injected under the skin overlying the ADM to provide a more natural feel and hide any rippling.

How should my wound look?
The other question that preoccupied me and to which I struggled to find an answer was how should a wound look three weeks after surgery? When I saw the surgeon two weeks post-op, he said my wound was looking marvellous, but how was I to know what to expect? I really scared myself during my parents' visit when it became infected. I was worried that by overdoing it, I might cause my implant to pop out through my healing wound. This is what happened to Alice-May Purkiss, who describes it in her book *Life, Lemons and Melons*. I found all sorts of gruesome pictures on the internet of wound dehiscence, implant loss, infection and other horrors. There's precious little guidance about what a normal

wound should look like. I came to the conclusion that rest is vital for ensuring a healthy implant.

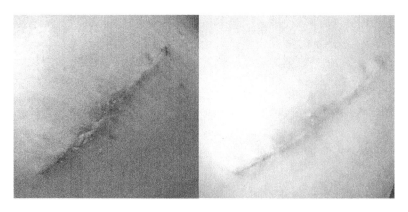

Left: Naughty wound seventeen days post op
Right: Nice wound five days later (after some rest!)

Resources

This is not an exhaustive list, but these are the resources I have found particularly helpful.

Breast Cancer
https://breastcancernow.org (biggest UK breast cancer charity)
https://www.cancerresearchuk.org (you can join their excellent Cancer Chat forum)
https://www.macmillan.org.uk (lots of useful resources here)
https://www.breastcancer.org (very informative US charity)
http://liz.oriordan.co.uk (brilliant blog by a breast surgeon who had breast cancer)
https://soulsafaris.com.au (my friend Merryn's meditations and retreats)
https://bigholeblog.wordpress.com (my own blog)
Life, Lemons and Melons by Alice-May Purkiss (fab book charting a young woman's experience of breast cancer as well as depression)

Mental Health
https://doctor-and-patient.com (thought-provoking blog by psychiatrist Rebecca Lawrence)
Depressive Illness: The Curse of the Strong by Tim Cantopher (one of the best books about depression I have read)
The Other Side of Silence by Linda Gask (autobiography of a psychiatrist's struggles with her own depressive illness)
https://www.rcpsych.ac.uk/mental-health (UK's Royal College of Psychiatrists' mental health resources page)
https://www.getselfhelp.co.uk/index.html (excellent cognitive behavioural therapy based site offering a myriad of self-help)

Involuntary Childlessness
https://gateway-women.com (Jody Day's community for women who are 'childless not by choice' has been a lifeline for me)

Printed in Great Britain
by Amazon

79877680R00129